Computer Communications

Robert Cole

Department of Computer Science,
University College, London

Springer-Verlag

New York

First published 1982 in the United Kingdom by
The Macmillan Press Ltd
Published simultaneously by
Springer-Verlag New York
(175 Fifth Avenue, New York, NY 10010, U.S.A.)
for distribution in the United States and its Dependencies

Printed in Hong Kong

Library of Congress Cataloging in Publication Data

Cole, Robert.
    Computer communications.

    (Monographs in computer science)
    Bibliography: p.
    1. Computer networks.   I. Title.   II. Series.
TK5105.5.C58   1982   621.3819′592   81–21321
ISBN 0–387–91204–5   AACR2

ISBN 0–387–91204–5

Contents

Preface

The subject of computer communications is changing very rapidly. Improvements in terminal access, aligned with the development of timesharing, has brought hands-on experience to a large number of non specialist users. Computer networks have made available vast computing resources and data banks to these users. This book is for anyone familiar with using computers who wishes to understand the techniques used in computer communications. It is also an introduction to the architecture of present day computer communication systems.

I would like to thank Roland Ibbett, Steve Treadwell, Peter Kirstein and Del Thomas for their invaluable advice and encouragement. My thanks also to Malcolm Stewart and the staff at Macmillan. The late Gareth Pugh encouraged my interest in computer communications and provided the opportunity to develop the material for this book. The text was formatted on a UNIX computer system: I am grateful to Professor Kirstein for permission to use this system. I am indebted to NEC Telecommunications Europe for the use of a spinwriter printer on which the master copy was produced.

Finally, no amount of words can express my debt to Jo and Rosemary for patiently bearing with this project over the last three years.

UNIX is a trademark of Bell Laboratories

1 Introduction

This text is concerned with the way computer-based information is transferred over long distances, and with the organisation of the communication system to meet various needs. A computer system usually consists of a CPU, memory, peripherals (on site) and communication devices. These are normally connected together by one or more short, high speed, data highways (figure 1.1). Computer organisation around the data highway is one of the topics of computer architecture. This book assumes the reader has some knowledge of computer system organisation and is familiar with using a computer. The subject of computer communications involves the problems and solutions of transporting data over distances longer than the internal computer data highway. For practical purposes we will treat a communications device as a piece of equipment that is used to transfer computer data to other equipment outside the computer room. There are exceptions of course: for example the computer console terminal may use communications techniques covered in this book, and some devices such as tape drives and large discs may be 'outside' the computer room. Figure 1.2 shows the various types of communication arrangements that will be covered. Each type of organisation and the techniques used for the device and the computer to exchange information will be dealt with.

The increase in the organisational complexity of computer communications reflects the trend in computing overall. Increased computing power, the cost of which is falling, is enabling the more efficient usage of resources, such as communications devices, the cost of which is rising. Even where communications costs are falling the cost of computing power is falling faster. This theme can be seen as a growing trend throughout the book. As all communications uses limited bandwidth channels, more and more complexity is added to the

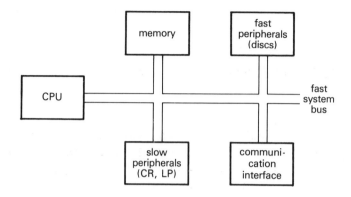

Figure 1.1 **Computer System Components**

communications system to obtain the maximum efficiency
from the communications channel. Increasing the system
complexity requires more computing power, but the cost
of extra processing is outweighed by the improved
efficiency of the system.

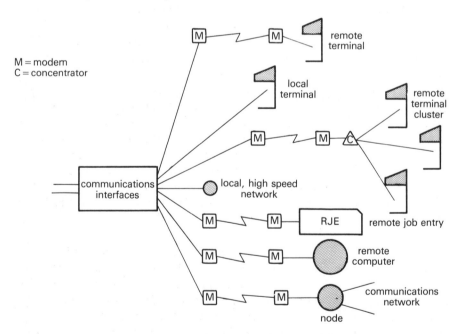

Figure 1.2 **Communications Systems**

This text uses a 'bottom up' approach, by explaining the basic principles of data communication and applying them to a physical application first, then covering more complex organisations and eventually reaching computer networks.

Throughout the book various different techniques are explained, and their advantages and disadvantages pointed out. The reader is asked to compare techniques and realise that there are situations where one technique is more useful than another but that full consideration should be given to all factors before deciding. The factors affecting the usage of various techniques are an important consideration of the book.

The text begins in chapter 2 by looking briefly at some transmission theory, mainly to establish that there is a limit on the rate at which information may be transferred in a medium, indicating that the medium is a resource which needs to be used efficiently. The use of wire as a medium is investigated as far as transferring characters is concerned. Chapter 3 looks at the particular problems of using the Public Switched Telephone Network (PSTN), and why the PSTN is so important in communications. Chapters 2 and 3 cover the use of the two most common media for actually transferring data. Chapter 4 goes on to look at the organisation of terminal networks and multiplexing techniques that can be used to optimise the use of a communications medium.

The use of messages rather than single characters as a unit of data transfer is taken up in chapter 5, which also introduces the idea of a protocol. Distributed computing as a part of communications is discussed briefly in chapter 5. The impact of errors and their unavoidability is pointed out in chapter 6, with the techniques used to try to discover and recover from errors. As most message-based protocols use a combined error recovery and flow control technique, the use of flow control is shown at the end of chapter 6.

The various technologies used in packet switched computer networks are introduced in chapter 7. Chapter 8 is concerned with with the X25 network access protocol. In chapter 9 the host–to–host protocols are introduced and some discussion of the host–network interface is given. Chapter 10 introduces some problems in computer network organisation by treating a network as a system and looks at techniques for optimising the system performance.

The text is designed as an introduction to the various techniques of computer communications, and the interested reader is encouraged to pursue the further details of the techniques. A bibliography of books and collections of introductory papers is given as a starting point for deeper study.

2 Transmission in Wires

The point at which computer communications and electronic data transmission overlap is in the transmission of data in wires. Virtually all computer communications involves the use of wire. The few exceptions are very high speed transfers using waveguides, optical fibres and radio frequencies.

To transfer information three components are needed: a sender, a receiver and a suitable medium. In this chapter we will concentrate on the principles of how to use a suitable medium for computer data communications.

2.1 Information Channel Theory

Waves are used to carry information through most media, especially those being used in real time. A book does not communicate in real time as the reader cannot respond by asking questions and the author cannot respond to the reader by attempting to answer them. A conversation is a real time communication. The simplest wave possible is the sine or cosine wave. Each wave has three characteristics: amplitude, frequency and phase.

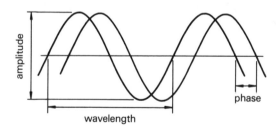

Figure 2.1 **Simple Signal Wave Components**

Figure 2.1 shows the simple wave and its components. Amplitude is an absolute measure of the height of the wave, the units depend on how the height is measured and in what medium it occurs. For instance a voltage wave

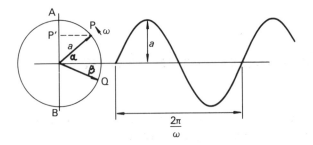

Figure 2.2 **Generation of a Simple Wave**

in a piece of wire would have its amplitude measured in
volts, a sound wave travelling through the air would
have an amplitude measured in millibars. The frequency
is an absolute measure − for our purposes it is the
number of times a wave shape repeats in a second. The
phase is a relative measure: it is the difference in
time between two waves. The phase difference of two
waves is normally given as an angle, as will be
explained later on. Amplitude, frequency and phase are
important in data communications because they are used
to code information using modulation, which is described
in the next chapter. To understand phase and frequency
in a simple wave look at figure 2.2, which shows how a
simple (sine) wave can be made by projecting a rotating
arm on to a plane.

Imagine that a chart recorder is moving through **AB**
and the pen marks the projection **P'** of the point **P**
moving round the circle at constant speed. Assume that
when the time (t) is zero **P** lies on the x axis
($\alpha = 0$ radians). If **P** rotates at a constant velocity of
ω radians/second then at any time t the angle α is

$$\alpha = \omega t \quad \text{radians} \tag{2.1}$$

The projection on to **AB**, which is drawn on our chart,
and shown on the right of the circle is (from equation
2.1)

$$a \sin(\alpha) = a \sin(\omega t) \tag{2.2}$$

When **P** has completed a revolution it begins to repeat the pattern, one revolution or cycle drawing a complete pattern or wave. One revolution consists of 2π radians; the time taken for that revolution is $(2\pi)/\omega$ seconds. The frequency of a wave is the number of revolutions in a second, which is the inverse of the time for one revolution

$$\text{frequency} = \omega/(2\pi) \qquad\qquad (2.3)$$

Now consider a second point **Q** which sets off at the same speed as **P**, and therefore has the same frequency, but at a point β radians away from **P**. The difference between the two waves is one of phase, **Q** is β radians out of phase with **P**. Phase can only be measured between two waves.

Any two simple waves having the same amplitude and frequency, and with a phase difference of zero are equal and indistinguishable. Information can be coded and transmitted in waves by changing the values of one or more of the components. Speech involves using frequency to get high or low sounds, amplitude to get loud or quiet sounds and combinations of amplitude, frequency and phase to make sounds, words and sentences carry information through air.

Information

At this point we should consider what is meant by information. The transfer of information between a sender and receiver is the purpose of a communication. Consider the analogy of sound: it is possible to hear sounds which have no meaning at all (they contain no information), apart from their presence. When we hear speech it usually means something, provided it is clear enough and in a suitable language. The purpose of computer communications is to transfer information between various pieces of computing machinery, though other signals not containing information may also be present. The term 'information' represents an abstract concept; for information to be transferred it has to be represented by something more substantial that can be carried. In computer communications, as in computers, the information is usually coded as patterns of bits.

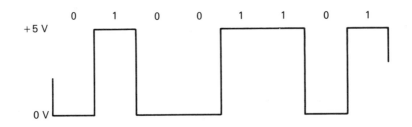

Figure 2.3   **Square Wave Coding of a Bit Pattern**

In a medium such as wire these bit patterns can be represented by voltages using only two values, say 0 volts and +5 volts. The use of two value signals leads to 'square waves', so called because when the signal changes it produces a characteristic 'square' shape when displayed on a graph or oscilloscope. Figure 2.3 shows a square wave and the information that it could represent.

A regular square wave is one that changes its signal level (or displacement) regularly with time. The frequency of a regular square wave is the inverse of the time between one signal level change and the next level change in the same direction. From figure 2.3 it can be seen that a wave carrying information does not change regularly but depends on the information. Usually the frequency of a square wave carrying data is the maximum possible number of changes, this is equivalent to data of alternate 1s and 0s (01010101...). A signal such as that in figure 2.3 is called digital because it has only a few values for the amplitude (in this case +5 V and 0 V). The term 'digital' distinguishes a square wave from a continuous wave called 'analogue'. The wave in figure 2.1 is analogue as it has a smoothly changing displacement. A square wave is a digital signal.

Square waves, and in fact waves of any shape, can be shown to be made up of simple sine and cosine waves, such as those in figure 2.1. Each constituent simple wave will differ from the others in its values of amplitude, frequency and phase. A square wave which repeats itself every second has a frequency of 1 Hz (Hz is the unit symbol for hertz; that is cycles or revolutions per second). Such a wave would be made up of simple waves having the following frequencies

$$1\,Hz + 3\,Hz + 5\,Hz + 7\,Hz + 9\,Hz \ldots \text{ to infinity}$$

As the frequency of the constituent waves increase the amplitude of those waves decrease, thus the higher frequency waves are not so important as the lower frequency waves.

Bandwidth

To transmit a perfect square wave it is necessary to be able to transmit an infinite number of frequencies through the transmission medium, but unfortunately this is not possible. All transmission media, senders and receivers, are limited in the frequencies they can manage. The range of frequencies that a piece of equipment or a medium can accommodate is called its frequency range; the difference between the highest and lowest frequencies is called the bandwidth. The bandwidth may be a physical property of the equipment or a limitation imposed for some reason. For example the human ear can only hear sounds in the range of approximately 20 Hz to 20 000 Hz, the actual values depending on the individual and age. The frequency range of the ear is then 20 to 20 000 Hz and the bandwidth is 20 000 minus 20. The range of the human ear is constrained by the physical properties of the ear. The telephone has a frequency range from 300 Hz to 3400 Hz − a bandwidth of 3100 Hz. The frequency range of the telephone is restricted by British Telecom for practical reasons.

If the bandwidth of the equipment or medium is restricted this means that some of the constituent simple waves that make up a square wave signal will not pass through the equipment or medium. As the constituent simple waves are removed in decreasing frequency order the square wave deteriorates, as shown in figure 2.4. If enough of the constituent waves are not allowed through a medium the received signal becomes unrecognisable. The result of this is that the transmission equipment and medium used to transfer information must have a sufficient bandwidth to allow a sufficient number of the constituent waves through to

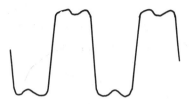

Figure 2.4 **Deteriorated Square Wave**

enable the receiver to recognise the signals correctly.
The actual values depend on how easy it is to recognise
the signals after transmission. The frequency range
requirement limits the frequency of any square wave we
can transmit through any medium; the higher the
frequency of the square wave, the higher will be the
frequencies of the important constituent simple waves
needed to represent the square wave, and the larger the
required bandwidth.

Capacity

Starting with the fact that a square wave is made up of
a number of simple waves, then adding the idea of
bandwidth, we come to an important conclusion: there is
a limit to the frequency of a square wave that we can
use in a particular communication system. The limit of
the equipment is determined by the frequency range
(bandwidth). Earlier, the frequency of a square wave
was associated with the number of changes in signal
level; if each **possible** change represents a piece of
information, then the limit in frequency is also a limit
on the the rate at which information can be transmitted.

It is possible to calculate theoretical limits on the
rate of information transfer, but first there is a
concept to be established. The medium used for
transmission is the physical equipment used to connect
the sender and receiver (say a piece of wire). The
medium will have a bandwidth, which, because the sending
and receiving equipment normally have much larger
bandwidths, will determine the information rate. (An
exception to this can occur in local networks where the
receiving and sending equipment are the bandwidth
limited components.) A channel is a path for

communication – it is a logical concept which is implemented in a medium and includes the sending and receiving equipment. A channel carries information in one direction (sender to receiver). A channel between the sender and receiver will have its own bandwidth and therefore its own information rate. Although the bandwidth depends on the physical medium, it can be artificially constrained as with the telephone system. Because the channel may be implemented in several media it is independent of them. It is now possible to discuss the communication path between the sender and receiver as a channel and discuss its implementation in various media separately. The next chapter considers the implementation of two channels on one medium (a full duplex MODEM).

Having separated the concept of channel from its implementation, the calculation of a maximum information rate can be confined to the channel. Remember that the channel exists between the sender and receiver – it represents all the equipment and media needed for that communication.

There is a relationship between the information being transferred down a channel and the maximum rate of transmission. Three factors affect the information rate

1. the method of encoding information

2. the number of distinct symbols which may be sent

3. the bandwidth of the channel.

If the information consists of **P** different symbols (for instance the letters of the alphabet) then the information content is

$$I = \log_2(P) \qquad \text{bits} \qquad (2.4)$$

If **P** is 128, the ASCII character set for example, then

$$I = \log_2(128) \qquad \text{bits}$$

$$I = 7$$

so 7 bits are needed to represent 128 different symbols, something that should be no surprise. The ASCII character set is dealt with in chapter 4.

The capacity of a channel is the maximum rate at which information can pass through the channel, that is the number of distinct symbols per second. If **T** is the minimum time to transmit one symbol, then

$$\mathbf{C} = 1/\mathbf{T} \qquad \text{symbols/second} \qquad (2.5)$$

This can be put into bits per second by multiplying **C** by $\log_2(\mathbf{P})$

$$\mathbf{C} = 1/\mathbf{T} \, \log_2(\mathbf{P}) \qquad \text{bits/second} \qquad (2.6)$$

It can be shown that the bandwidth of a channel (measured in hertz) is $1/(2\mathbf{T})$ therefore

$$1/\mathbf{T} = 2\omega \qquad (2.7)$$

(ω is the bandwidth); so

$$\mathbf{C} = 2\omega \log_2(\mathbf{P}) \qquad \text{bits/second} \qquad (2.8)$$

Unfortunately this equation is only true for a perfect channel; it is impossible to make such a thing, so the equation has to be modified to allow for noise. The noise represents the imperfections that reduce the information rate. For instance during a conversation there are often interruptions when the speaker has to repeat what was previously said, the interruptions are a form of noise that reduces the rate of information transfer. Claude Shannon modified equation 2.8 to allow for noise; this is now called Shannon's equation.

$$\mathbf{C} = \omega \log_2(1+S/N) \qquad \text{bits per second} \qquad (2.9)$$

S/N is the signal to noise ratio. The signal to noise ratio for a channel is usually given in decibels. A decibel is a ratio between two values, in this case the power of the signal (S) and the power of the noise (N) disrupting it. The S/N ratio in decibels is given by

$$\text{decibel value} = 10 \log_{10}(S/N) \text{ dB} \qquad (2.10)$$

(dB is the unit symbol for a decibel.)

Example 2.1

What is the maximum information rate (channel capacity)
of a channel which allows frequencies between 300 Hz and
3300 Hz?   The channel   has   a   signal   to   noise   ratio
measured at 20 dB.   (These are approximate values for a
telephone   line,   which   is   introduced   in   the   next
chapter.)

First,   find   S/N   as   a   simple   ratio,   using   equation
2.10

$$dB = 20 = 10 \log_{10}(S/N)$$

$$S/N = 100$$

(that is the signal is 100 times more powerful than the
noise); the bandwidth is $3300 - 300 = 3000$ Hz
From Shannon's equation $C = \omega \log_2(1+S/N)$

$$C = 3000 \log_2(1+100)$$

$$C = 3000 \{\log_{10}(101) / \log_{10}(2)\}$$

using $\log_n(V) = \log_m(V)/\log_m(n)$

$$C = (3000 \times 2.00432) / 0.30103$$

$$C = 19,963 \quad \text{bits per second}$$

Getting the answer in bits per second is very useful
for computer communications as computers work in, and
transmit, bits as their basic unit of information.   The
result of the above calculation is very misleading – the
signal to noise ratio of 20 dB is an **average**.   Sometimes
the the noise is very high compared to the signal and at
other   times   it   is   very   low;   sometimes   only   some
frequencies   are   affected.   The   implication   is   that
although   an   average   noise   ratio   of   20 dB   would   not
result in much data being lost, a higher value would, so
when   the   noise   peaks,   a   lot   of   data   is   lost   and   the
capacity goes down.   This problem of 'bursts' of noise
is   taken   up   in   chapter 6,   under   error   detection   and
correction.   The   bandwidth   given   above   is   also   an
average (on a telephone line the equipment making up the
connection for a call may change for every call) so the
bandwidth   can   change   as   well.   In   fact   it   is   not
possible to use the whole frequency range (300 to 3300)
for   various   technical   reasons   associated   with   telephone

equipment. The problems of using telephone equipment for digital data communication are taken up in the next chapter.

It is now obvious that the amount of information that can be transferred in a certain time is limited. This leads to a need to make efficient use of equipment to ensure that as much data as possible is transferred up to the available limits. This pressure for efficiency will arise over and over again as we discover, not surprisingly, that faster transfer rates cost more money and therefore need to be justified in a commercial environment.

The theoretical considerations discussed so far need some practical application. How can bits of information be transferred through a medium such as a length of wire? So that not too much reliance is placed on one type of medium, the discussion is in terms of waves, which are then given a physical representation suitable for a particular medium, such as wire.

2.2 Channel Organisation

The first problem to be overcome is the number of bits to be transferred at the same time. If several bits are transmitted at the same time then several channels will be needed, for instance several pieces of wire. This is called parallel transmission, as the channels and the data are in parallel. Parallel transmission is used extensively within the computer to transfer data from one section to another at very high speed. A whole unit of information (word, byte, etc.) is transferred at once, taking only one unit of time. However there are problems in parallel transmission that get worse as the distance between the sender and receiver increases.

1. COST – As each bit transferred needs its own channel, to transfer several bits in parallel means providing several channels, for instance several wires, senders and receivers. As the distance increases the cost of the channels becomes high.

2. SKEW - Not all channels have exactly the same
   characteristics; one of the important differences is
   the speed at which a wave can travel in a channel,
   which is particularly pronounced in wires. The
   differences are mainly due to tolerances in the
   components. In parallel channels, even if all the
   signals representing data are transmitted at the
   same time, the signals do not arrive at the receiver
   at the same time because they all travel at
   different speeds. Figure 2.5 shows the idea of skew
   in parallel wires. As the distance between the
   sender and receiver increases so the skew increases.

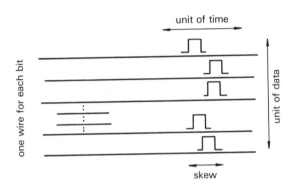

Figure 2.5   **Skew in Parallel Transmission**

Within a computer system the emphasis is on
transferring information as fast as possible over very
short distances, so the problem of skew is reduced and
the cost is not so important as the speed. For long
distance communication between computer systems
(distances of perhaps several kilometres) the problem of
skew becomes very noticeable and parallel transmission
is very expensive. These problems can be eliminated by
using serial transmission though some disadvantages are
introduced. With serial transmission, units of
information are sent one after another on the same
channel, one information unit in one time unit. Serial
transmission will require 8 time units to transfer 8
bits of data, but only one channel is used, whereas with
parallel transmission 8 bits could be transferred in 1
time unit but 8 channels would be needed.

To implement one channel requires two wires to make a complete electrical circuit. In an 8 bit parallel bus a ninth wire is used as a return wire to make the circuit for all eight of the data-carrying wires. With a serial system a return wire is still needed, the other carries the information signal.

Currently most computer communication involves wires; certainly in that part of the physical communication that computer personnel are concerned with, the use of wires will continue for some while yet. Advanced technology, such as fibre optics, will be used increasingly in data communications when standards for them have been agreed and accepted.

A fibre optic link has a much larger bandwidth than an electrical wire link. It is not prone to electromagnetic noise so it will have far more capacity and be less likely to allow corruption of data from noise than a wire.

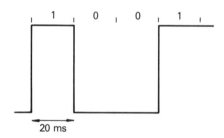

Figure 2.6   **Two-level Code**

Coding Data in Signals

Information has to be coded into the signals transmitted through the communications medium. There are many different coding techniques used in data communication: for instance, if in one time period we wish to transmit one of two different symbols (say 1 and 0) then we could use two values of amplitude in a square wave, see figure 2.6. This means we are transferring 1 bit of information in 1 time unit. In figure 2.6 each symbol takes 20 ms (milliseconds = 10^{-3} seconds). If 1 bit takes 20 ms then in 1 second 50 bits will have been transmitted and the information rate is 50 bps (bits per

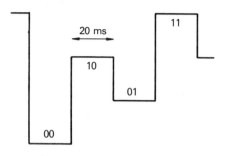

Figure 2.7 **Four–level Code**

second).   Another term that is used by communication
engineers to describe an information signal is 'baud'.
Baud is used to measure the signalling rate, or the
number of times the signal may change in a second.   In
figure 2.6 the signal may change at the end of each bit
time, or every 20 ms.   Therefore the signalling rate for
figure 2.6 is 50 baud, or 50 possible changes a second.
To send one of four different symbols (say 00, 01, 10
and 11) in one time unit we could use four values of
amplitude as in figure 2.7.   Notice in the figure that
each symbol still takes 20 ms so the symbol rate is
still 50 per second, and that the baud rate is twice the
maximum   possible   frequency   (that   is   data   of
01010101...).   To encode four symbols we use 2 bits for
each symbol so the information rate is now 100 bps.   The
baud rate for figure 2.6 is still only 50 baud as the
signal can only change every 20 ms.   The term baud is
really only of use to the communications engineer.
Unfortunately   it   has   been   misunderstood   by   some
computing people and made synonymous with bits per
second to describe the data rate of a channel or piece
of equipment.   Where one symbol is represented by one
bit then the baud rate and bps value are the same
(figure 2.6) but if the symbol is represented by more
than 1 bit then the baud rate and bps value are
different (figure 2.7).   More complex communications
devices are likely to use multilevel signals such as
those in figure 2.7.   The term bits per second (bps)
will be used throughout to describe information rates
and the term baud will only be applied to signalling
rates.

There are three modes of operation between two communicators using channels

1. simplex – this is a connection where one party can send information to the other, but no information can be transferred in the reverse direction. There is only one sender and one receiver and one channel.

2. half duplex – in this arrangement both parties can send and receive information, but not at the same time. The communications channel only allows information transfer in one direction at any time. This uses one channel, but the direction is reversed by switching between sending and receiving equipment at each end.

3. full duplex – both parties can send and receive information at the same time. This uses two channels.

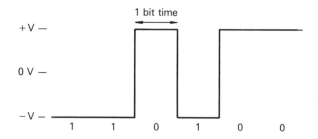

Figure 2.8 **V24 Information Coding**

Bit Coding in Wires

Having established the requirement for transferring a serial stream of information along a channel, a method of encoding data into electrical signals for use in wire can now be considered. The most common coding method is a voltage amplitude system which has been adopted as an international standard. The standard is often referred to as V24 because it is part of a specification of an interface between computer communications equipment that is called V24. The international V24 standard is the same as RS232C which is the name used in the United

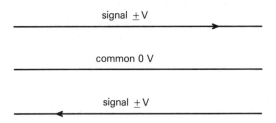

Figure 2.9 **Three-wire V24 Full Duplex Connection**

States, and on equipment manufactured there.
International standards are discussed briefly in section
3.3. Here only the voltage levels used to transfer data
are discussed; the whole V24 specification covers all
the data and control signals needed to connect terminal
equipment to MODEMs and other communications devices.

As computer data is confined to bits, it is only
necessary to distinguish between '0' and '1' as symbols.
The two voltages chosen to represent these symbols are
+V to represent a '0' and -V to represent a '1'. The
value of V may vary between 3 and 24 volts. The +V
value is called a 'mark' and the -V value is called a
'space'; a common arrangement is to use +12 and -12
volts. Figure 2.8 shows the bit pattern 110100 as it
would be transmitted over 6 bit times using V24 signal
levels. If the signal voltage is 0 volts or completely
absent, then the line is in a 'break' condition which
usually means the power is off, or the 'break' key has
been depressed on the terminal. Remember that two wires
are needed to transmit an electrical signal, so there is
one wire carrying the signal voltage; the other wire
remains at 0 volts as the return wire. If we wish to
return information in the opposite direction (full
duplex), then a third wire is needed to carry the
reverse direction signal voltage. As both circuits can
share the 0 volt line (called common), shown in figure
2.9, each signal carrying wire represents one channel.
Most interactive terminals connected to an in-house
timesharing computer normally only use these three wires
to transfer characters between the terminal and the
computer.

Simplex and half duplex only require two wires for an electrical circuit; full duplex requires three wires using the V24 communication encoding.

2.3 Character Framing

Now that the signal encoding techniques have been explained it is necessary to organise the information so that it can be transmitted and recovered by the receiver. Since most computer communications concerns the use of character devices, such as terminals, printers card readers etc., the basic unit of information used for organising the data transfer is the character. The bits sent as electrical signals are packed as characters for the basic unit of transfer. The receiver has to be able to recognise a serial stream of bits as characters, that is to detect the start of a character and its end, then by implication the start of the next character. In this context a character is a number of bits, where the number remains constant during a communication. There are two character framing techniques for recognising and separating characters from the serial bit stream

1. asynchronous framing - without a common clock, characters can be sent and therefore received at any time.

2. synchronous framing - with a common clock, characters are sent continuously at a specified rate.

The speeds and applications of these two character framing methods are shown in the table below.

Asynchronous	Synchronous
mechanical terminals slow printers 75 to 300 bps	buffered terminals intelligent devices remote job entry 2400 to 19200 bps
unbuffered terminals (VDUs) 300 to 9600 bps	computer to computer >9600 bps

Transmission line speeds (in bits per second) are not chosen at random but come from an internationally agreed list of preferred speeds (75, 110, 300, 600, 1200, 2400, etc). Most communications devices are capable of working at a range of these preferred speeds.

Asynchronous Character Framing

A user sitting at a terminal (teletype or VDU) will type characters at an indeterminate rate and there will also be periods when no characters are being typed. The terminal will receive a few characters from the computer and there will be an interval while the user thinks about them. In either case the receiver (either the terminal or the computer) does not know when the next character is going to arrive, nor how many characters there will be. To meet these problems the asynchronous framing technique puts the character into a frame consisting of a start bit and a stop bit. Figure 2.10 shows the letter 'A' in an asynchronous frame, using the ASCII code discussed in chapter 4. The bits are transmitted (and received) from right to left.

When there are no characters to transmit the signal voltage is kept at −V (normally about 12 volts). Then, when a character is ready for transmission (say a key on the keyboard has been pressed), the voltage is changed to +V and kept there for 1 bit time. This is called the start bit. After the start bit the bits that make up the character are transmitted by using the appropriate voltage, +V for a '0' and −V for a '1', and holding the voltage for one bit time. After all the bits for that character have been sent, the transmitter sends a stop

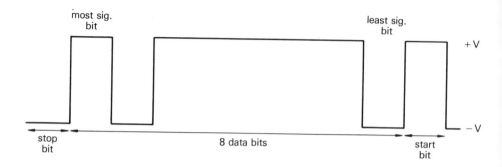

Figure 2.10 **Asynchronous Character Frame**

bit by holding the voltage at −V for at least 1 bit time before beginning the next character.

The start bit warns the receiver that a character is arriving, the −V to +V change is used by the receiver to start a local clock to read in the bits of the character. In this way the local clock is resynchronised for each character. The stop bit has two functions, neither of which is concerned with marking the end of the character.

1. On mechanical terminals, usually those with a transmission speed of 110 bps, 2 stop bits are used to allow the mechanical parts to get ready for the next character.

2. By having the last bit at −V, it ensures that the −V to +V change of the start bit will be properly recognised, regardless of the last data bit in a character.

The two devices (terminal and computer) have to agree on

1. the number of bits in a character− this may vary from 5 to 8

2. the bit time; this is set up by deciding how many bits per second to transmit, a 300 bps connection has a bit time of 0.0033.. seconds.

The number of stop bits is another parameter but there

are acceptable defaults: a 110 bps connection would have
2 because it is usually a mechanical teletype; the other
speeds have only 1 because they are usually used with
VDUs. If in doubt about stop bits the sender should use
2 and the receiver should expect only 1.

Synchronous Character Framing

Asynchronous character framing is designed for the
situation where the characters are transmitted
intermittently. There are situations where larger
volumes of information need to be transferred, such as
whole files to and from a remote job entry station or
between computers. To transfer the larger volumes of
data higher speeds are used. Synchronous framing is
used where a number of characters or blocks of bits are
to be transferred. It involves transmitting characters
continuously, that is there is always a character being
transmitted and received. Obviously the sender and
receiver have to use the same transmission rate (bps)
and the same number of bits per character, though this
is usually 8.

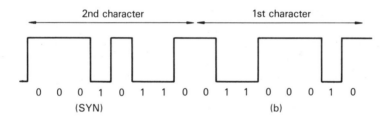

Figure 2.11 **Synchronous Character Framing**

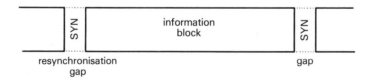

Figure 2.12 **Synchronous Transmission Blocks**

Synchronous character transfer using serial transmission means that all that appears in the channel is a continuous stream of bits; figure 2.11 shows the arrangement. At the receiving end the bits need to be combined into characters, so the first bit of the character has to be found. The problem of 'synchronisation' over characters is solved by using special characters. When the transmitting equipment is switched on a continuous stream of a known character, such as the ASCII SYN (00010110 binary), is transmitted. When the receiving equipment is switched on a stream of bits will be received. By shifting the bits until the SYN character is recognised the character boundary can be found, then the next frame of bits should be the next character. The synchronous frame size is the number of bits in a character. Using this technique the character frame can be found within two character frames being sent from the transmitter. During information transfer the characters are collected by counting the bits which in turn are found by using a local clock. This local clock has to be synchronised with the local clock at the sender, hence the term synchronous transfer. Over a period of time the clocks tend to become unsynchronised and data may be lost if the bits are not correctly interpreted. To overcome this problem the communications channel has to be resynchronised at frequent intervals. This is done by splitting the data into blocks and sending a few SYN characters in between the blocks. The use of blocks is important in error control and flow control which are discussed in chapter 6, and of course the information within the computer is often organised into blocks. Figure 2.12 shows the blocking arrangement. Usually 8 bits are used for each character in a synchronous transfer. This size has had a strong impact on the arrangements (called protocols) used to transfer information between computers; this is discussed later.

Synchronous and asynchronous framing techniques are used to pack bits into 'characters' as the smallest unit of transfer, and as most communication is based on printing characters this is not unreasonable. The mapping of the groups of bits into particular graphic characters used for printing is quite arbitrary; each character should be considered as a bit pattern which is interpreted by other equipment.

2.4 Send and Receive Equipment

Within a computer system the information is transferred in parallel, so a device is needed to take bits from the computer data highway, in parallel, and transmit them in serial using the appropriate character framing method. A similar device is needed to receive characters in serial, check the frame, collect the bits and pass them to the computer in parallel. Fortunately there are large scale integrated circuits that perform all of these functions. There are three separate devices: one for asynchronous framing, one for synchronous framing, and one (often used with microprocessors) which can handle both types of framing, though not at the same time.

The device for use with asynchronous framing is called the UART (Universal Asynchronous Transmitter and Receiver). It performs the serial to parallel conversion, frame generation and checking; it can be programmed for 5,6,7,8 bit characters, parity (even, odd, or none) and any line speed using an external clock. There is a similar device for synchronous transfer called a USRT (Universal Synchronous Receiver and Transmitter).

A block diagram of a UART is shown in figure 2.13. Because the USRT is very similar a description of the UART will suffice. The following description of the UART operation should also help to clarify character framing techniques.

When a character is to be transmitted the bit pattern is loaded in parallel from the computer into the transmitter buffer register. This is then transferred to the transmitter register when the transmitter register is empty. Whilst one character is being transmitted from the transmitter register the next one can be loaded into the buffer register so that continuous transmission is possible. Once the data is in the transmitter register a start bit is transmitted, followed by the

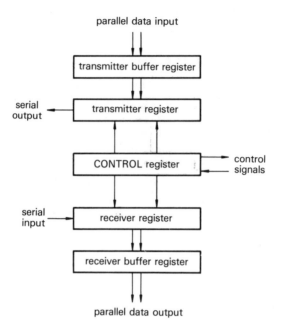

parallel data input

transmitter buffer register

serial
output   transmitter register

CONTROL register   control
signals

serial
input   receiver register

receiver buffer register

parallel data output

Figure 2.13 **UART – Block Diagram**

bits of the data (character), which are shifted out bit
by bit, one bit in every bit time. When the character
has been shifted out the stop bit is added, and the next
character, if any, can be loaded from the buffer
register. The UART uses a clock rate of sixteen times
the bit rate, so that if a transmission rate of 300 bps
is required the clock needs to be 4800 Hz. The need for
a faster clock is more obvious when considering the
receiving function.

When a character is to be received the UART is warned
of its arrival by the −V to +V voltage change on the
input. Immediately this occurs a counter is set to 8
and then counted down at every clock pulse. As there
are 16 clock pulses to every bit time, this counter
reaches zero half way through the start bit. If the
voltage is still +V at this time it is assumed that a
character will follow, otherwise the logic is reset and
and error bit set on the computer interface. After the
first sample half way through the start bit the counter
continues, modulo 16. This means that every time it
becomes zero the middle of the next bit should be at the

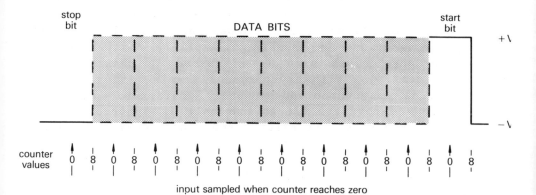

Figure 2.14 **UART Receive Clocking**

input. The value of each bit is found by sampling the input every time the counter reaches zero. The technique can be improved by taking a number of samples (say 4) around the middle of the bit time; then averaging the samples. The average is then compared against a threshold values. This improvement is particularly useful in a noisy environment. By using a clock rate of sixteen times the bit rate the centre of each bit can be found quite accurately. After the expected number of bits have been sampled the next sample should be the stop bit. If this last sample is not −V a frame error is indicated on the computer interface as the asynchronous frame has not been completed properly. The most likely cause of a frame error is that the transmitter clock at the other end was not running at the same speed as the receiver clock. In other words the sender is using a different bit rate from the receiver. Some computers use this frame error to try to match the line speed to that of the terminal, this is called 'automatic bit rate detection'. Figure 2.14 shows the receive clocking arrangement.

2.5 Comparison of Character Framing Techniques

The major operational difference between the two character framing techniques is in the synchronisation method. With the synchronous frame the receiving clock, and therefore the character frame, is resynchronised with the received bit stream for every block of characters, so the sender and receiver clocks are always in synchronisation. Each block may contain a large number of characters, depending on how often synchronisation is needed. Another constraint on synchronous block size is discussed in chapter 6 on error control. With asynchronous framing the receiving clock is resynchronised on every character. Thus the sender and receiver clocks are only in synchronisation during character transfer, and then only for that character.

The difference in the two techniques is due to the type of communication required. Where the information is in small units, say one or two characters, and the transfer is intermittent, with arbitrarily long periods of idle, then the asynchronous technique is used. The major use of the asynchronous frame is with terminals connected to computers for interactive use. Because of the requirement to resynchronise on every character, the asynchronous frame has 2 extra bits for every character. Assuming an 8 bit character, then only 80% of the bits transferred are the information the sender wants the receiver to get. The other 20% (start and stop bits) are redundant as far as the information is concerned, though necessary for the safe transfer of the information. If characters are transmitted continuously, at the maximum rate allowed by a channel using an asynchronous frame, then only 80% of the channel capacity is being used for useful information, the other 20% is overhead.

Where there is a requirement to transfer a large amount of information, it will be transmitted continuously by using the synchronous character frame technique. For example, if a block size of 96 characters is used and four extra characters are used to separate the blocks for resynchronisation, then the efficiency for each block is 96%. This is higher than that possible for asynchronous character framing.

2.6 Summary

This chapter has introduced some of the basic ideas of communications and the nature of computer data communications. The limitations of a communications channel and how it may be used to transfer computer data

have been explained. A wire as a communications medium
was used as an example as nearly all present computer
communications uses electrical signals and wires. The
most important result of the communications theory is
that **the rate of transmission of information is limited
by the bandwidth and noise of the communications
channel.**

The information to be transferred has to be coded
into signals, for instance as electrical voltages for
use in wires. The smallest unit of information is a
'bit'. Most computer communication systems group the
bits into fixed size characters as the basic unit of
transfer. Two character framing techniques were
introduced: synchronous for continuous transfer, and
asynchronous for intermittent transfer of characters.
The synchronous technique is useful for large volumes of
data, but does not cope with intermittent traffic. The
asynchronous technique handles intermittent traffic well
but is inefficient for large volumes of data.

3 The Telephone Network as a Medium

The previous chapter made the distinction between the medium used to carry information and a channel which is a logical path from sender to receiver through which the information is passed. A channel is implemented in one or more media. Probably the most important communications medium for computer communications is the telephone system.

3.1 The Telephone System

Terminals, remote batch stations, and even other computers can easily be attached to a computer in the same locality can be done easily by laying down some wires. However when longer distances are involved two problems arise.

1. Over a long distance the electrical signals are attenuated, that is they lose power and become unrecognisable.

2. In most countries it is illegal for private individuals or companies to transmit data outside their own property.

The first problem is an electrical one so it is not covered here; however it is well to be aware of it.

The second problem is more intractable and is the source of considerable contention. The constraint on data transmission is due to a monopoly on the telephone service. In most countries the telephone system is operated by licence. This licensing arrangement means that certain individual companies or a government agency, such as British Telecom (formerly part of the British Post Office), are granted a licence to provide and operate a telephone system.

Most countries have a government body to run the telephones: in the United Kingdom British Telecom operate this monopoly. In the United States a number of private companies are given licences by the Federal Communications Commission (FCC) which oversees the arrangements. Such licensees are known as common carriers in the USA. The effect of the monopoly given to the licensees is that only the licensee can erect systems (of wire or otherwise) to carry signals such as telephone conversations, or computer data.

The licensees are usually called PTTs (PTT stands for Postal, Telegraph, and Telephone authority) and this reflects the arrangements more common in the rest of the world rather than the USA. In economically advanced countries the PTTs have established a comprehensive network of telephone connections specially designed to carry speech. This network is called the Public Switched Telephone Network (PSTN). Even if the PTTs did not have a monopoly it would make sense to try to use this existing network for long distance computer data communications, as all the cables are readily available.

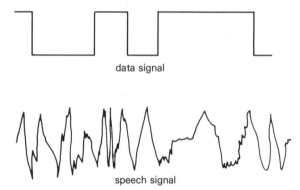

data signal

speech signal

Figure 3.1 **Comparison of Speech and Digital Signals**

The major problem with the PSTN is that it was designed before anyone even thought of computers. The telephone system is ideally suited to carry speech where a human being can concentrate on decoding the received sounds and try to understand them. There are a number of factors contributing to the PSTN being a poor medium for the type of signals discussed in chapter 2, however.

Firstly, the equipment has a frequency range of 300 Hz to 3400 Hz, which is not very wide for high speed data traffic. Secondly, the frequency range is not continuous, some frequencies may be used to operate equipment at exchanges. Phone freaks in the USA can make calls by whistling into the telephone handset and causing the exchange to set up the call. If a data wave produces the wrong frequency the call may be disconnected. This problem is taken up in the section on modulation. Finally, to protect the exchange equipment from damage no DC current is allowed through the local exchange. By looking at the type of wave produced by speech against a data signal, in figure 3.1, it can be seen that the speech signal never has the same voltage continuously, whereas the data signal consists almost entirely of a continuous voltage at one of two levels. The continuous voltage is the DC (direct current) part which would be removed by the exchange. Removing the DC part would seriously distort a digital data signal.

The PTTs provide three solutions to these problems

1. Special equipment to convert digital data signals into audio signals which can easily be transmitted through the PSTN.

2. Private four–wire connections to the local exchange, then a fixed circuit to the remote site. This cuts out some parts of the PSTN that cause problems, but not all of them.

3. Direct links of high bandwidth most of the way between sites.

Each of these solutions represents increasing cost, but results in a higher information rate.

Solution 1 – This involves the use of a MODEM (MOdulator DEModulator) on the ordinary telephone line that converts the binary signals into audio signals and back again. Only one two–wire circuit is used, but the

available bandwidth is divided to provide two channels;
one in each direction. One medium – two channels.

Solution 2 – When the bandwidth in solution 1 is
insufficient, an extra two wires are added, and all the
wires permanently connected. This means that some of
the lost frequencies can be used.

Solution 3 – Because of the way the telephone exchanges
are connected together, solution 2 does not normally
require special connections between exchanges. However
when a very high bandwidth connection is needed, say
50K bps, then some extra inter-exchange connections have
to be made. If special connections are made right
through, then modulation techniques may not be required.

A normal telephone handset is connected to the local
exchange by two wires, which is sufficient for an
electrical circuit. The subscriber can dial any other
subscriber on the PSTN by passing through the local
exchange. At the exchange connections are established
through a hierarchy of other exchanges. The exchanges
are connected together by wideband channels which are
subdivided into smaller channels; each small channel is
sufficient for one call. The subdivision uses a
technique called frequency division multiplexing which
is explained in chapter 4. When a call is connected the
caller is allocated a series of small channels between
the exchanges through to the subscriber that is being
called. The subscriber can dial-up any other subscriber
only by passing through the local exchange which sets up
the connection.

The first solution above allows a subscriber to
dial-up anywhere and then transfer data by using
equipment that will pass data signals through the
exchange. This equipment, a slow MODEM, does not have a
very high data rate: 300 bps full duplex or 600/1200 bps
half duplex. To improve the data rate (by reducing the
error rate and increasing the available bandwidth) the
local exchange has to be bypassed, but this means the
dialling facility is lost. Normally British Telecom
provide a four-wire connection bypassing the exchange
with a small channel permanently allocated through to

the destination. This through connection is called a private circuit as it can only be used by the two subscribers, one at each end. Different MODEMs can be used on private circuits to provide a faster data rate on the better bandwidth. The noise levels on a private circuit are normally lower than on a dialled connection, (remember Shannon's equation).

The third solution is used to provide a faster data rate. For this, direct connections bypassing several exchanges are made so that the required bandwidth and noise level can be obtained.

All of these three methods use some of the existing telephone system. British Telecom are now introducing a special data transfer network which is designed for computer data, but uses as many of the existing methods as possible. This new network, known as PSS (Packet Switching Service), uses techniques described in chapters 7, 8 and 9.

The interested reader might like to refer to the POST OFFICE/NCC book (see bibliography) for more details of how the British PSTN works.

The major piece of equipment needed to transfer data through the PSTN is the MODEM. Modulation is a technique that can enable information signals to be passed through a medium not really suited to them.

The original, and still the major, use of modulation is in radio transmission. By using that analogy it is possible to see how modulation can be used to pass digital data signals, such as those in figure 2.8, through a medium designed to carry voice signals. The human voice does not travel very far on its own, and if more than one person were to try broadcasting (shouting) at the same time it would be very difficult to separate out the messages. The frequency range of an original signal is called the base band: for the human voice a base band of 300 to 3300 Hz is used on the telephone though a wider range is possible. When two people talk at once close together, they confuse listeners because they are both using the same frequency range, the base

band. To transmit speech over long distances very much
higher frequencies have to be used, and care must be
taken to ensure that different frequencies are used for
each different transmission. The original base band
frequencies have to be increased and no two
transmissions should use the same frequency range. The
only problems now are how to increase the frequency of
the base band signal without losing any information in
the signal, and then how to recover (or receive) the
original signal so that the transmission can be heard in
the base band. The problems are solved by modulation.

Modulation, very simply, involves superimposing the
information signal onto a simple carrier signal in such
a way that one, or more, components (amplitude,
frequency, phase) of the carrier are modified to carry
the information.

3.2 Modulation Techniques

This discussion is only related to techniques currently
used in MODEMs on the PSTN.

Frequency Shift Keying (FSK)

The digital data is recoded as frequencies. The binary
signal, such as V24 voltage levels, can only have two
values, so only two frequencies are needed. This
technique is used on slower MODEMs. In FSK the two
values of voltage are converted into one of two
different frequencies; this is done by a modulator. The
electrical circuit 'modulates' the input voltage to
produce the output. The receiver performs the opposite
process, it takes in the frequency signal and
'demodulates' it to produce the original voltage signal.

Using this technique on the telephone lines is fairly
easy, the frequencies can be in the range 300 to
3300 Hz so they are easily passed through the PSTN just
as if they were speech signals. The major problem lies
in the choice of frequencies for which there are a
number of constraints.

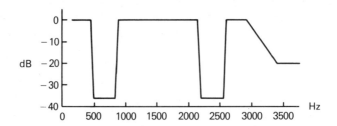

Figure 3.2   **PSTN Frequency Response**

1. The chosen frequencies have to be fairly far apart
   on the frequency range. That is, the cycle time for
   one should be measurably different from the other.

2. In order to detect the actual frequency, **at least**
   half a wave, or cycle, must be transmitted. This
   means the input digital wave cannot change faster
   than twice the lowest frequency output from the
   modulator. Thus the lowest frequency used must be
   greater than the baud rate of the data signal.

3. Certain frequency ranges on the telephone circuit
   are reserved for use by the switching equipment
   (these are internationally agreed, so even if a PSTN
   does not use them they cannot be used for
   modulation).

4. The higher frequencies on a telephone circuit are
   attenuated.

Figure 3.2 shows the frequencies which can be
transmitted on the PSTN. The gaps represent the
forbidden frequencies, the slope at the higher
frequencies indicates the attenuation. Any frequencies
chosen for use in MODEMs are usually agreed
internationally so they will operate in all countries
that are party to the agreement. The CCITT co-ordinates
these agreements. In section 3.3, on MODEMs, the actual
frequencies are given. Figure 3.3 shows the range of
frequencies used by MODEMs at various data rates.
Notice how the faster MODEMs use wider frequency ranges;
this is a result of Shannon's equation which shows that
a higher data rate needs a higher bandwidth. The wider
range used by faster MODEMs is also partly due to the

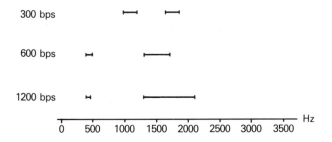

300 bps

600 bps

1200 bps

0   500 1000 1500 2000 2500 3000 3500   Hz

Figure 3.3 **MODEM Frequencies**

need to choose frequencies that do not interfere with
each other. Frequency shift keying is an important
concept in modulation techniques for digital data
communications, but is limited by the low frequency
range of the PSTN. Frequency signals are also
susceptible to noise, such as that from a mains cable
which has its own frequency (the hum that can be heard
from some hi-fi systems).

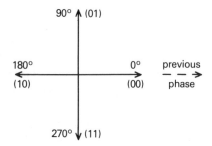

Figure 3.4 **Differential Phase Modulation Encoding**

Phase Modulation

A newer technique that is used to provide a higher
information rate whilst using the same frequencies
involves coding the data into the phase of a wave.
Remember that phase is measured between two waves; it
can also be measured between the same signal wave at
different points in time. If a wave has phase p_1 at
time t_1, we can measure the phase at time t_2 relative to
the phase at time t_1. It is very difficult to measure
small changes in phase, so MODEMs mainly use large
changes.

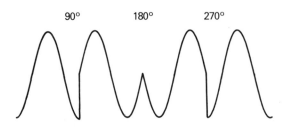

Figure 3.5 **Phase Changes**

The technique known as differential phase modulation is shown in figure 3.4; there are four possible phase changes (0°, 90°, 180°, 270°) so each possibility represents 2 bits of data. A continuous frequency simple wave is used so that only the phase component changes; figure 3.5 shows the phase changes. To be able to detect the phase changes a complete wave, or cycle, is used. In any one cycle there are four possible changes that could occur, so each cycle represents 2 bits of information. For instance, if we use a frequency of 1200 Hz we can have an information rate of 2400 bits per second. A problem can arise with the phase encoding shown in figure 3.4: if a stream of zeros is transmitted, no phase change occurs during that time so the receiver and sender (modulator and demodulator) can become out of bit synchronisation. To overcome this an alternative differential phase modulation encoding scheme is used on newer MODEMs. The alternative coding is shown in figure 3.6. Notice that every code now has a phase change from the previous cycle, enabling the bit synchronisation to be maintained.

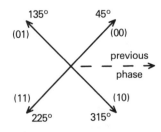

Figure 3.6 **Alternative Phase Modulation Encoding**

Quadrature Amplitude Modulation

This modulation technique combines changes in phase with different signal amplitudes. The data is encoded into a specific phase change and signal amplitude. For instance if there are four possible phase changes and each one can be paired with one of two different signal amplitudes, then there are now eight different combinations giving 3 bits of information in each baud. This idea is being used on the faster MODEMs above 2000 bps to increase the information rate without increasing the signal frequency. The amplitude of a signal is more likely to be changed by noise than the frequency or phase, so it is not very suitable for use as a modulation parameter for data communication on its own. Figure 3.7 shows an example of amplitude and phase encoding.

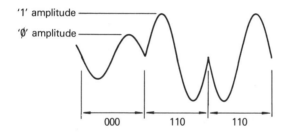

Figure 3.7   **Amplitude and Phase Modulation Encoding**

3.3 The MODEM

This section describes three MODEMs to illustrate the practical arrangements made to use the PSTN for binary data using the modulation techniques previously described. The frequencies mentioned are standard CCITT recommendations, they are not the same as those used on some MODEMs in the US.

A Timesharing Terminal MODEM

A timesharing terminal is restricted by the typing and reading speed of a human being, and as such it has a relatively low data rate. The terminal also needs a full duplex connection. The MODEM used to provide the timesharing terminal with a connection to a remote

computer divides the bandwidth on the PSTN into two
parts to provide two channels. Normally this MODEM is
connected to an ordinary telephone line, allowing the
user to dial any computer he wishes, but of course this
means passing through the local exchange using a two-
wire circuit. The timesharing MODEM uses frequency
shift keying to implement the two channels; the
frequencies are

channel 1	binary 0	1180 Hz
	binary 1	980 Hz
channel 2	binary 0	1850 Hz
	binary 1	1650 Hz

Modem A

channel 1 modulator
channel 2 demodulator

Modem B

channel 1 modulator
channel 2 demodulator

Figure 3.8   Initial MODEM Channel Usage

If channel 1 is used by one MODEM to transmit on a
connection it must be used by the other MODEM for
receiving, and vice versa. The timesharing MODEM can be
used at either end of a connection, terminal or
computer. A mechanism is needed to decide which channel
should be used for transmitting and which channel for
receiving at each end. By international agreement the
following mechanism is used. When a MODEM is switched
on, but before being connected for a data transfer, it
is set to transmit on channel 1 and receive on channel
2; this is shown in figure 3.8. One of the MODEMs in a
connection pair must change if data transfer is to
proceed: by agreement this is the MODEM associated with
the called computer or terminal. The normal situation
is for the computer MODEM to be called by the user.
Where a MODEM may be used to receive a call, such as at
a computer site, the MODEM is arranged so that the

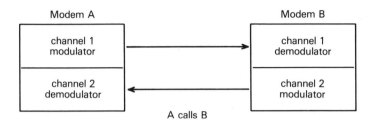

Figure 3.9 **MODEM Channels After Connection**

incoming call switches the called MODEM over. Figure
3.9 shows two MODEMs after the connection has been
established.

    This type of MODEM arrangement is the most commonly
used; it has been arranged so that a device known as an
acoustic coupler can be used to replace the caller's
MODEM. An acoustic coupler does not need installation
directly into the telephone system. An acoustic coupler
uses the same frequencies as the ordinary MODEM, but
instead of placing them directly onto the telephone line
it whistles into the mouthpiece of a telephone handset
and takes the received signals from the earpiece. The
acoustic coupler is a very cheap and convenient way of
connecting a terminal to any telephone. Unfortunately,
using the handset allows other noises from the room to
interfere, so it is not as reliable as an installed
MODEM.

Higher Speed Asynchronous MODEM

Sometimes a faster rate of data transfer is required,
say for printing messages, though the input may still be
slow. The bandwidth available on the PSTN is not
sufficient, given the noise, to allow a full duplex
connection faster than 300 bps. However, research is
continuing on modulation techniques to achieve faster
data rates. A second type of MODEM is used to provide a
higher speed in one direction, but a much lower speed in
the other direction. Up to 600 bps can be guaranteed on
the PSTN in the UK, passing through the exchange in one
direction, whilst the return channel has only 75 bps.
The return channel is called a supervisory channel and
is not expected to carry much data. Up to 1200 bps may

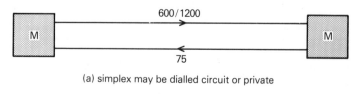

(a) simplex may be dialled circuit or private

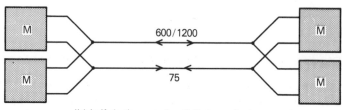

(b) half duplex may be dialled or private
circuit

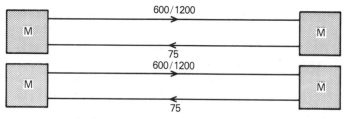

(c) full duplex (requires a 4-wire circuit)

Figure 3.10   **600/1200 bps MODEM Arrangement**

be obtained using a dial-up connection if the noise is
very low, but a private circuit will provide a
guaranteed 1200 bps. If a connection of 600/1200 bps is
needed in both directions then two MODEMS are needed at
each end. If the PSTN is used via a dial-up line only a
half duplex connection is possible, because the circuit
can only manage 600/1200 bps in one direction at a time.
If a private four-wire circuit is used then a full
duplex connection is possible. Because the direction of
the main data transfer is fixed, one type of MODEM is
used for sending on the fast channel (600/1200 bps) and
receiving the supervisory channel (75 bps), whilst a
different model performs the reverse operation at the
other end (figure 3.10). The 600/1200 MODEM uses
frequency shift keying as the modulation technique, with
the following frequencies

Up to 600 bps	binary 1	1300 Hz
	binary 0	1700 Hz
Up to 1200 bps	binary 1	1300 Hz
	binary 0	2100 Hz

The receiving MODEM can always tell if the sender is using 600 or 1200 bps as the idle frequency (binary 0) is different for the two data rates. Note that the frequency range 1300 Hz to 2100 Hz fills the middle of the available frequencies on the PSTN (figure 3.2). This means that the supervisory channel is relegated to using the low frequencies, and therefore has a low data rate. The frequencies for the supervisory channel are

	binary 1	390 Hz
	binary 0	450 Hz

Fast Synchronous MODEM

A popular speed for synchronous transfer is 2400 bps. This is provided by a group of MODEMs that use differential phase encoding to obtain the higher data rate within the frequency range of the PSTN. The connection pattern is the same as for the 600/1200 bps MODEM; a simplex connection is available on the two-wire circuit via the exchange with a sending and receiving MODEM. If a sending and receiving MODEM are provided at each end, a half duplex connection can be made by sharing the two-wire circuit. A full duplex connection can be obtained by using a private four-wire circuit. A 2400 bps MODEM is available for use over the PSTN using a dial-up line, but may be limited to 1200 bps by noise. The 2400 bps main data connection can be augmented by a 75 bps supervisory channel in the reverse direction, as in the 600/1200 MODEM. The differential phase encoding uses four possible phase changes on a 1200 Hz signal to obtain the 2400 bps data rate. MODEM speeds of 4800 bps and 9600 bps are also available, but only using private circuits.

Very High Speed MODEMS

For use in inter-computer communications an arrangement is available for data rates between 40.8K bps and 50K bps over 48 kHz wide band circuits. Some of the larger exchanges in the PSTN are connected by very wide band circuits. These can be utilised for data transfer, although a private high speed circuit may have bypassed several exchanges on the way to the large exchange. For the high speed circuit four MODEMS are used, one pair to reach the large exchange, and another pair at the other end. Between the end pairs of MODEMs the data is passed in the base band frequency of the data signals on a special (and therefore more expensive) private circuit. This arrangement is used for connecting packet exchanges in a wide area packet switching network which is discussed in chapter 7. The four-MODEM arrangement is shown in figure 3.11.

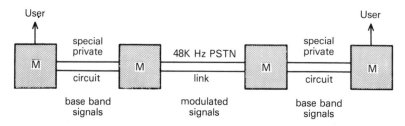

Figure 3.11   **Four-MODEM Arrangement**

The main uses of MODEMS are listed below.

1. Connect a teletype or slow VDU (110/300 bps) to any computer in full duplex, by dialling through the PSTN. (Solution 1 in section 3.1)

2. Connect a faster terminal (600/1200 bps), but to get a full duplex connection a permanent private circuit is needed, so only one computer can be used. (Solution 2 in section 3.1)

3. Provide a synchronous connection using higher data rates (1200/2400, 4800, 9600 bps) but again a private circuit is needed for full duplex and full speed operation. (Solution 2 in section 3.1)

4. A very high data rate can be achieved, but at a higher cost, using base band signalling for part of the distance on a special circuit. (Solution 3 in section 3.1)

In terms of cost the acoustic coupler represents the cheapest modulation equipment. The cost then rises through the four types of MODEM described above. The higher the data rate, the higher the cost; however the relationship is not linear. A 1200 bps service does not cost four times as much as a 300 bps service: it is more likely to cost only about twice as much to install, especially if a private wire is needed, but the rental may only be half as much again. Thus the problem of obtaining the optimum cost/service is not easy.

3.4 Digital Data Network

So far in this chapter we have been concerned with using an analogue PSTN that was designed to carry speech signals. The PTTs are currently investing very large sums of money in converting the existing (and in many cases old) analogue telephone equipment to use digital technology. In the UK, British Telecom are installing System X in a number of new exchanges and gradually replacing old exchanges and equipment.

The new digital systems convert the analogue speech signal into digital signals using a technique called pulse code modulation. The encoded speech signals are carried through the network as digital signals and converted back to their analogue form for the receiver. Using digital signals for transferring analogue information has a number of advantages.

1. The effects of noise are considerably reduced.

2. Digital multiplexing techniques can be used to make more efficient use of the trunk network.

3. The subscriber circuits can be switched by digital processors (computers) using information embedded in the encoded signal.

4. The very cheap VLSI technology developed for computers can be used, thus allowing considerable intelligence to be built into the telephone network.

A further advantage for users of computer communications is that the PSTN can be used directly, and therefore more efficiently. The digital information from the computer is passed directly into the digital network where it is transferred in its original form.

System X uses a circuit of 64 kHz bandwidth as its basic unit; compare this with the 3.3 kHz currently used on the analogue PSTN. Eventually every telephone in the UK will be connected by a 64 kHz circuit; thus opening tremendous possibilities for personal information services.

The (comparatively) high bandwidth of the digital network will have a big impact on computer communications when the network is widely available. Some digital services are already available from the West German PTT and some US common carriers.

3.5 Standards

The PTTs from all over the world work through a body called the CCITT (International Consultative Committee for Telegraphs and Telephones is the English translation of the French title). The CCITT is a part of the United Nations. It is concerned with enabling the individual PTTs from all over the world to co-operate and provide an international service. The CCITT is the most authoritative standards organisation in communications so any standard adopted by the CCITT is very important.

All of the MODEMs discussed in this chapter conform to international standards for their operation, so it is possible for a terminal user in the UK to use a timesharing computer in Germany by dialling the computer. The German computer uses a German MODEM, the UK user has a UK MODEM, but because they conform to the same standards they will be able to operate together (noise on the international call permitting). The CCITT have had a tremendous impact on computer communications

by standardising various interfaces between computing
equipment. The most important interface is that between
the MODEM (which is usually supplied by the pttΔ and the
user's   equipment.   For   instance,   for   asynchronous
terminals the interface standard is called V24. The V24
standard defines all of the control and data signals
used to enable the MODEM and the user's equipment to
operate together and pass data, including the signal
levels.   The data signals shown in figure 2.8 are in
fact only a small part of the V24 specification which
covers the data signals.

The result of the standards and their widespread
adoption by equipment manufacturers means that any
terminal having a V24 interface can be plugged into any
MODEM, anywhere. Furthermore computer manufacturers now
use the V24 standard for connecting local terminals as
well.   This compatibility between equipment is very
important in allowing various different types of
equipment,   from   different   manufacturers,   to   be
interchangeable.   Because   the   manufacturers   in   the
United   States   dominate   the   computer   industry   the
standards adopted by the United States often become the
international standards of the CCITT.   One of the US
standards called RS232C is in fact the same as the V24
recommendation and preceded it.   RS232C was the name
given to the standard in the US before it became an
international recommendation.   Many US manufacturers
still refer to it as RS232C rather than V24.   (There are
some differences between RS232C and V24 concerning a few
control functions, see the book by McNamarra for a
detailed comparison.)

The CCITT have defined a standard interface for
connecting communications equipment to a digital
switched network: this standard is known as X21. A
second interface standard, known as X21(bis), allows the
same mechanisms but over the analogue PSTN; because
there are still so few digital services available. The
packet switched network access interface, X25, is
defined to used X21 as its lowest level. However,
X21(bis), or even V24, may be used where a digital
network is not yet available.

A serious user of computer communications should be aware of the CCITT and its V and X series recommendations.

3.6 Summary

Long distance communication has a problem in the monopoly given to the operators of a PSTN. This monopoly has resulted in a large amount of computer data communication being forced to use the PSTN. The problems in using the PSTN are due to its being designed to carry human speech and not digital data. Using modulation a number of techniques have been designed for transporting data across the PSTN at various price/performance levels. The adoption of standards, promoted by the PTTs has led to compatibility between various pieces of computing equipment and encouraged the widespread use of communications facilities.

4 Character Terminal Networks

The two previous chapters have covered the problems of transferring information as a serial stream of bits, partitioned into groups called characters. The primary motivation for grouping the bits into characters, rather than say computer words, was the early need to communicate between character-oriented devices such as teletypes, displays, printers and the computer. The growth of interactive computing has led to the widespread use of networks of computer terminals connected to a central computer. The purpose of this chapter is to look at the network organisation used for asynchronous terminals.

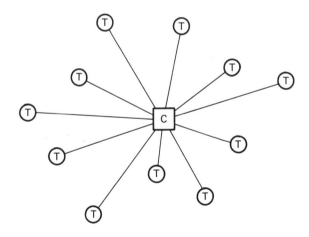

Figure 4.1 **Star Network Topology**

The majority of timesharing computers that are used from interactive terminals operate on a character by character basis using a full duplex connection. There are two basic network arrangements used for asynchronous terminals.

1. **Star network**

This arrangement provides each terminal with its own physical connection to the main computer; it is shown in figure 4.1.

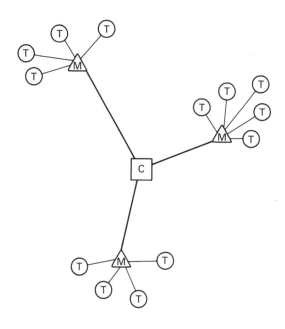

Figure 4.2   **Remote Multiplexer Network Topology**

2. **Remote multiplexer network**

Each terminal has a connection to the nearest remote multiplexer, then it shares a connection to the computer with other terminals, as in figure 4.2.

The choice of connection is governed by cost/performance constraints.

   The object of a timesharing computer is to provide a service to each user, usually at a terminal, such that the user thinks he is the only user of the computer. The terminal network has to support this illusion by attempting to make the remote terminal appear to be attached directly to the computer. The major criterion in this illusion is the response time. A designer of a terminal network will attempt to provide the best response, which means the highest information rate at

the lowest possible cost. Response and cost are the
criteria to be borne in mind in the discussion on
terminal networks. So far the discussion on information
transfer has been limited to bit patterns. In chapter 2
the bit patterns were grouped as 'characters' but there
was no discussion of what a character meant. When using
a terminal the user is confronted with a keyboard
containing recognisable characters. On the screen, or
paper, similar characters will appear: these are called
graphic characters as they can be printed. There are
functions such as a new line, back space, or tab that
are represented by control characters, as they control
the operation of the terminal. Each character is mapped
into a particular bit pattern, so that as the user
depresses a key the terminal will produce the
appropriate bit pattern and send it as a character unit
to the computer. At the computer the bit pattern will
be inspected to try to discover which key was depressed
and therefore what action is required. If the user
presses the key marked 'A' then it is useful if the
computer recognises the resulting bit pattern as the
character 'A'. To achieve this a standard mapping is
required between the graphic characters, the control
characters and the bit patterns actually transferred.
Such a mapping is called a character code.

4.1 Character Codes

The description above emphasises the need for a common
understanding between two parties in a communication.
Such an understanding is called a protocol. The use of
the asynchronous character frame and V24 voltage levels
is a protocol. Without protocols communication is
impossible. It is important to realise that every
standard (such as V24) is just a widely accepted
protocol that enables widespread communication. The
further use of protocols is taken up in later chapters.

There are two main character codes that have been
adopted: they are ASCII (American Standards Committee
for Information Interchange) and EBCDIC (Extended Binary
Coded Decimal Interchange Code). The ASCII code is
named after the committee in the United States that
first proposed it; EBCDIC is a product of IBM and is
used on their equipment. A third code called IA5

(International Alphabet number 5) is the standard of the CCITT. IA5 is almost exactly the same as the ASCII code except that it allows for one or two local variations such as different currency signs. The IA5 code is also the standard recommended by the International Standards Organisation (ISO).

The ASCII code has been adopted by most computer manufacturers outside IBM influence. It is a 7 bit code, with no parity recommendation. 7 bits allows for 128 different symbols of which about 93 are graphic characters and 35 are control characters. The IA5 code is based on ASCII but uses even parity to produce an eighth bit. For most terminals the two codes are exactly the same; the eighth bit is often ignored.

The EBCDIC code is an 8 bit code invented and used by IBM. As a manufacturer IBM has sufficient domination of the computer market to have its own standards and not worry too much if they differ from everyone else's. The EBCDIC code covers nearly the same graphic and control characters as ASCII, but there are a number of the 8 bit patterns that are not allocated as character codes.

Some computer manufacturers have their own internal character codes, left over from days before standards were available. This means that the standard bit patterns have to be converted before they can be understood by the computer software, and of course converted back for communications use. Nearly all terminals available now use either ASCII or EBCDIC as their code.

There are other less well-known codes using as little as 5 bits per character. In computer communications the use of standards has nearly eliminated these except on old equipment.

4.2 The Star Arrangement

The requirements to connect a single terminal to the computer are listed below.

1. A terminal with a UART

2. A communication medium

3. A UART at the computer end

4. An interface between the UART and the computer internal communication system (for example the bus).

A UART does not actually produce the V24 signal level voltages discussed in chapter 2; a second integrated circuit is needed to take the serial I/O from the UART and convert it to the V24 voltage signals. The use of a second chip merely allows the UART to be used with any voltage signalling system. A computer terminal usually comes complete and ready to plug into whatever medium is to be used. The plug would be standard, usually the V24 standard 'D' plug. A computer manufacturer will supply an interface containing a UART and a signal level converter which plugs directly into the computer. It comes with a standard plug ready to be attached to the communications medium. The medium could be, at the moment, either a length of wire or a PSTN connection involving two MODEMs. Figure 4.3 shows the units as they are obtained. All the buyer of the arrangement has to do is

1. Ensure the computer interface and the terminal are provided with compatible interfaces (V24)

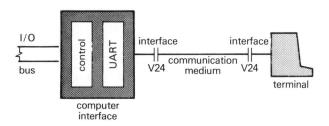

Figure 4.3 **Components of a Terminal Interface**

2. Provide a suitable medium, wire for an in-house connection, or a PSTN connection with MODEMs for an external connection.

If MODEMs are used the purchaser should ensure that the terminal and interface plugs are for MODEM use which is always a V24 (RS232C) standard.

In the remainder of this chapter 'suitable medium' will mean either an in-house wire, or PSTN connection, depending on the installation requirements. The use of the 'D' plug with the connections and signals arranged in the V24 standard now means that any terminal or computer can be attached to any medium using the standard connectors.

Connecting a single terminal is reasonably easy, but connecting a large number, say one or two hundred, is slightly different. The obvious approach with a star network would be to use one computer interface for each terminal. As all the terminals are separate, each will have its own medium. However, a large number of interfaces on a computer causes problems in physically fitting them in, addressing each interface and other considerations of speed and efficiency within the computer. One solution adopted is to use a local multiplexer. Multiplexing is a technique which enables several inputs onto one output; the reverse operation is called demultiplexing. A multiplexer normally performs both functions. The terminal multiplexer is a device made by the computer manufacturer to enable several terminal lines to use one interface to the computer. The assumption is made by the designer of a terminal multiplexer that an asynchronous terminal will not be used continuously for very long, and even when a continuous stream of characters is being transferred the transfer rate will be very low compared with the capacity of the computer interface. A common number of terminals to put on a single local multiplexer is 16; thus if each one has a transfer rate of say 1200 bps (which is too fast to read and understand by a human) then the total worst case rate is $16 \times 1200 = 19\,200$ bps. A bus on a minicomputer could transfer over 1 million bps, so there is plenty of spare capacity in the computer for other transfers.

The multiplexer uses one UART for each terminal line and from the outside looks like a number of individual terminal interfaces, but there is only one computer interface for all of the UARTs. Where each terminal has its own computer interface the computer software can identify each terminal, and therefore the user, by the address of the interface. But when several terminals are using the same interface each terminal needs another address within the interface. Figure 4.4 shows how several terminals are arranged when connected via a local multiplexer interface. Each terminal has its own port which consists of a UART and the signal level converter. The local multiplexer performs the function of multiplexing the terminals via the single computer interface. A common mode of operation of the multiplexer is to use a scanner register to address each UART in a round robin sequence. The register is incremented as a modulo n counter where n is the number of terminal lines on the multiplexer. For this reason n is usually a power of 2 (8 or 16) as this makes implementing the counter easy. As a new number comes up in the scanner register the corresponding UART is tested to see if there is a character waiting in its receive buffer. If so, the character is removed and the present contents of the scanner register are added to make a line number/character pair. In this way each UART is given an address within the multiplexer and every character associated with that port is tagged by the port number. After any received character has been dealt with, the multiplexer will look to see if there is a character to be sent out to the port; if there is, it is fetched (usually from the computer memory) and placed in the UART transmitter buffer register. The multiplexer scanner register is then incremented and the process repeated for the next port. As the scanning mechanism is implemented in hardware the whole process is very fast. The mechanisms by which characters are sent and received across the interface to and from the computer vary from computer to computer. Some manufacturers have more than one type of asynchronous

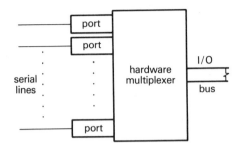

Figure 4.4 **Local Terminal Multiplexer**

terminal multiplexer to provide different levels of complexity at different prices.

4.3 Remote Multiplexers

A star network consists of a number of terminals, each having its own suitable medium up to the computer interface which will be either a single line interface or a local multiplexer. A timesharing computer would have a combination of single line interfaces and local multiplexers to suit the exact needs of its users within the constraints imposed by the manufacturer's hardware. As each terminal has its own dedicated connection, all the bandwidth of the connection (computer interface, suitable medium, terminal) is available for information transfer. When the terminal is idle, then the connection and connection equipment is idle. If some terminals are at remote sites then the MODEM and the telephone charges for each line may become very high. As many timesharing systems have more physical terminals than the number of active terminals they can support, some connections will be idle for long periods.

The PTT's pricing policy for MODEM charges (installation and rental) is such that a 2400 bps MODEM will cost only a little more than a 300 bps MODEM. So it makes economic sense to use the faster MODEMs if the total information rate justifies it. The star network is the obvious and natural first attempt at a terminal network design as it uses the simplest hardware and provides the best response. However if three, or four, or even more slow MODEMs can be replaced by one fast one, then the economics may justify a more complex network design. The use of remote multiplexers enables such a design.

The operation of a local multiplexer was described as enabling several terminal lines to interface to a computer via a single interface. The remote multiplexer enables several terminal lines to use a single high speed communications line. In figure 4.2 a number of terminals are connected by local PSTN lines or directly by wire to a remote multiplexer. The multiplexer is connected by a single high speed line to the computer. The multiplexer is 'remote' from the computer and very often involves a PSTN connection. There is no economic advantage in replacing a star network of local terminals connected by wire, only in replacing remote connections using the PSTN. The remote multiplexer has essentially the same function as the local multiplexer, except that its single high speed side is serial. Using a remote multiplexer is more expensive in terms of equipment, because a computer interface is still needed and the remote equipment is extra. The choice of design is made by weighing up the extra capital cost of the equipment (for remote multiplexers) against the savings from renting a few high speed lines instead of a large number of slow speed lines from the PTT. Other factors are involved of course. For instance, a PTT is more likely to provide a couple of high speed lines on time rather than say 100 slow speed lines, as each line has to be individually supplied. A commercial timesharing bureau may decide to use a remote multiplexer in an area or town so that its customers need only pay local call charges by dialling-up the nearest multiplexer, rather than the computer which may be a long distance away.

Remote Multiplexing Techniques

The techniques used for multiplexing are quite simple: they are concerned with sharing the bandwidth of the fast communications channel amongst the slow terminal lines on the 'other side' of the multiplexer. The difference between multiplexing and concentration is difficult to separate as some techniques fall into both camps. There are two situations to consider.

1. Input and output capacities are the same.
   Figure 4.5 shows a simplified case where a
   multiplexer has three slow speed terminal lines
   attached to it with a single high speed channel to
   the computer. If the capacities (line speeds) of
   each line are C_1, C_2, C_3 for the slow speed lines
   and C_f for the high speed channel. Then

$$C_1 + C_2 + C_3 \leq C_f \qquad (4.1)$$

if the high speed channel is to meet our
requirement. The inequality ($\leq$) is a practical
consideration as the actual line speeds may not
allow equality. For instance if
$C_1 = C_2 = C_3 = 300\,\text{bps}$ then $900 \leq C_f$. As 900 bps is
not a standard speed the actual value would be the
next standard speed which is 1200 bps.

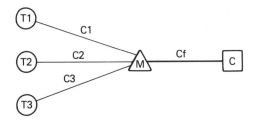

Figure 4.5   **Simple Multiplexer Arrangement**

2. The input capacity exceeds the output capacity.
   From figure 4.5 this means that

$$C_1 + C_2 + C_3 > C_f \qquad (4.2)$$

This is possible on a remote multiplexer with
terminals, as the terminals are never used
continuously because of thinking time and slow
typing rates. So there are periods when each
terminal line uses none of its capacity. What must
be assured is that C_f is large enough for the
average information rate on the terminal lines.
Denoting $\bar{c}$ as the average rate this gives

$$\bar{c}_1 + \bar{c}_2 + \bar{c}_3 \leq C_f \qquad (4.3)$$

for figure 4.5.

The situation in case (1), equation 4.1 above, is usually called multiplexing; the situation in (2) as described by equation 4.3 is usually called concentration. The situation described by equation 4.3 can only be implemented by equipment sharing a channel and cooperating over its use. Concentrators use storage to even out fluctuations in the actual transfer rates. Usage of these terms by various groups of people within the computer industry has led to some ambiguity in their meaning in the communications context.

There are two ways of dividing the bandwidth of the fast channel

1. Frequency division multiplexing (FDM), and

2. Time division multiplexing (TDM).

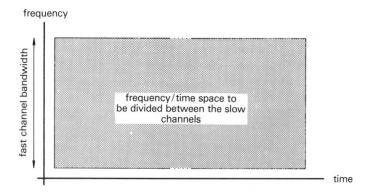

Figure 4.6 **Parameters for Multiplexing on a Channel**

Frequency division multiplexing is not used directly by computer communications equipment. It is used on the PSTN, and is described here in order to provide another illustration of the idea of multiplexing. Figure 4.6 shows on two axes the important features of the fast channel that has to be shared. Over a period of time it is required to share the bandwidth of the fast channel amongst the slower channels. The two multiplexing techniques are concerned with division along one of the axes.

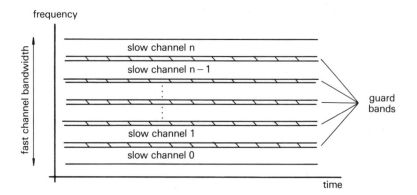

Figure 4.7 **Frequency Division Multplexing**

Frequency Division Multiplexing

By definition, the slow channels must have a narrower
bandwidth than the fast channel. Frequency division
multiplexing divides the frequency range of the fast
channel into a number of narrower channels, each of
which has the same bandwidth as a slow channel (figure
4.7). In between each allocated band of frequencies is
a guard band which is used to separate the narrow band
channels and avoid interference between them.

   Frequency division multiplexing has certain
characteristics which are worth noting.

1. Each slow channel has a permanently allocated
   (narrow) channel on the fast channel.

2. If the slow channel is not being used at any time
   the corresponding channel on the fast line is
   wasted.

3. The slow channels have to be modulated up to the
   required frequency slots, and demodulated at the
   other end.

Frequency division multiplexing is useful for systems where the channel is in continuous use. For this reason FDM is used on the PSTN to carry a number of telephone connections on the high speed channels used to connect telephone exchanges. Further information can be found in the Post Office/NCC book.

Time Division Multiplexing

The nature of computer communications makes the division of the high speed channel along the time axis very easy, and more efficient. The information is always transferred in characters which are of fixed length (usually 8 bits). The time axis is divided into slots: each slot is of sufficient time to transmit a single character. The whole bandwidth on the high speed channel is used to transmit the character so it can be transmitted much more quickly than on a slow speed channel. Figure 4.8 shows the bandwidth/time allocation in slots. If there are n slow speed channels connected to the multiplexer then the time slots are allocated to each slow speed channel in turn, so that every nth slot contains a character from the same slow speed channel.

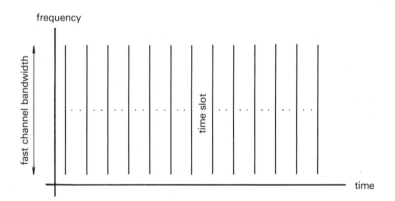

Figure 4.8   **Time Division Multiplexing**

There is no problem of receiving characters and deciding which terminal (slow channel) they belong to. The sender and receiver synchronise the slots by an internal mechanism, such as the use of SYN characters discussed in chapter 2. After the sender and receiver on the high speed channel have synchronised the slots, the first character (in the first slot) will be for the first slow speed channel, the second for the second slow speed channel, and so on. When the last slow speed channel character has been received in its slot, a character for the first slow channel is received next.

This multiplexing technique has some advantages for character-based computer communications due to the fixed size of the basic unit of information transfer, the character. Ordinary TDM still has some of the disadvantages of FDM though, in particular characteristic (2). If any slow channel does not have a character to send when its slot becomes available, perhaps because the user is thinking, then the slot remains empty in the high speed channel. Usually a null character of zeros is sent in this case. This means that some of the bandwidth of the fast channel is wasted. However the whole frequency range of the high speed channel is used as there is no wastage in guard bands. A multiplexer used with asynchronous terminals on the slow channels will always have empty slots as there are usually some terminals not active; the percentage of time a character terminal is actually sending or receiving a character is quite small. More complex techniques have been devised, based on ordinary TDM, which use the fast channel more efficiently when interactive terminals are used on the slow channels. These techniques, described below, cross the boundary between multiplexing and concentration though they still have the title 'multiplexing techniques'.

Intelligent or Statistical Time Division Multiplexing

With intelligent or statistical TDM the time axis is again divided into fixed slots; however the slots are not allocated on a round robin basis, but on a first-come first-served regime. As soon as a character arrives from a slow channel it is placed in the next free slot. This method raises two problems

1. How does the demultiplexer at the other end know which slow channel any character came from?

2. What happens if there is no free slot?

The first problem is easily solved: the time slot is lengthened to take extra bits which identify the slow channel. For instance a time slot of 16 bits could be used, as shown in figure 4.9. This allows 7 bits for the slow channel number, 1 bit as a control bit, and 8 bits for the character. Remember the fast channel would probably be a synchronous connection so allocating the slots in units of 8 bits is a good idea. The control bit can be used to identify this slot of 16 bits as a character. If it is 0 say, or if the control bit is 1, then the other 15 bits may contain control information passing between the multiplexer and demultiplexer at opposite ends of the fast channel. As the slots are not allocated to a fixed slow channel, it is easy to slip in control information about the status of the various slow channels for instance. It is possible to have variable sized slots; in that a number of characters from the same slow channel are grouped together and sent as a unit preceeded by some control information. Other complex framing schemes can be used, especially when a microprocessor is used to provide the intelligence in the multiplexer.

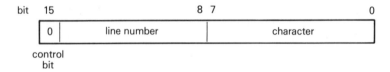

Figure 4.9   **Example ITDM Character Frame**

The second problem may be solved by some form of storage to hold the character until a slot is free; in this sense the intelligent multiplexer becomes a concentrator. The problem may also be solved by placing controls on the number and speed of the slow channels and then throwing away any characters that cannot be accommodated.

This type of multiplexer relies on the sum of the average transfer rates for the slow channels not exceeding the capacity of the fast channel. The statistical multiplexer requires more intelligence than an ordinary time division multiplexer, and with the introduction of control information the equipment is capable of much more sophistication in error handling and traffic control, hence the term 'intelligent'. This type of multiplexer is usually built around a microprocessor.

The choice of ordinary multiplexers or the intelligent type is a matter of economics. In terms of connecting more slow speed channels onto the same high speed channel the intelligent multiplexer is better, but will cost more. The low price of microprocessors as a source of intelligence with the better performance and more sophisticated control has in fact meant that most remote multiplexer networks use intelligent (statistical) multiplexing techniques.

4.4 Multiplexer Networks

The use of multiplexers shown in figure 4.2 is a very simple one. A system using remote multiplexers requires an interface device at the computer to receive and send characters to the remote multiplexers and interface in an appropriate way to the computer itself. Sometimes a high speed direct memory access interface is used to reduce the load on the computer for character output to the terminals. Since the network is character based, the interface sends and receives the characters separately, which in the worst case may mean an interrupt for every incoming character on some computers! Even with a high speed interface the processing required to handle the throughput of characters from an asynchronous terminal network can be very high. Many computers that have a terminal network use a front end processor (FEP) to handle the network and remove a lot of the character processing overhead from the main computer system. All of the local terminals and multiplexers will be interfaced to the FEP, which is usually a minicomputer. An FEP provides a number of advantages.

1. It can handle all character echo

2. It can edit lines before passing them to the main computer (for example rubouts, deletions and line editing)

3. When the main computer is down the FEP can be used to print a message to the terminal user,

4. The FEP can perform monitoring and statistics collection on the network performance.

The front end processor communicates with the main computer through a shared processor memory area, shared disc or high speed I/O channel.

With the extra processing power and flexibility of the FEP very complex networks can be designed using cascaded multiplexers for remote terminals, and star arrangements for local terminals. Cascaded multiplexers are used to save line charges by connecting multiplexers in series. In figure 4.10 the multiplexers A,B,C are cascaded. The high speed line for B needs to have the capacity to carry traffic from multiplexer B as well as the traffic from multiplexer C. The cascaded arrangement is cheaper in terms of line cost than connecting multiplexers B and C directly to the computer site. Usually cascaded multiplexers are of the intelligent type.

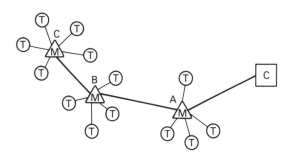

Figure 4.10   **Example of Cascaded Remote Multiplexers**

4.5 Designing an Asynchronous Terminal Network

The choice of equipment and the planning of a connection layout is not easy for an asynchronous terminal network. The usual constraints are the number and position of the terminals and the position of the computer. Terminals local to the computer that do not need PSTN connection are best attached by a star arrangement as this is cheapest and gives the best performance for the terminal user. Terminals needing a PSTN connection require more careful consideration. If only a few lines are involved a star arrangement may be cheaper; where a larger number are involved the saving in line rental by using a remote multiplexer will become more attractive. The cross over between a star design and a remote multiplexer has to be worked out for individual cases and must take into account other factors such as PSTN line availability and the facilities offered by the multiplexing equipment. For instance, to use remote multiplexers, a local multiplexer-demultiplexer is needed at the computer site. Often this multiplexer interface will also support local slow speed terminals directly, enabling the entire network to use a single computer interface. An example is shown in figure 4.11. The siting and choice of exact numbers of multiplexers to be used in a network design is an interesting exercise in its own right; interested readers can find more information in the book by Schwartz.

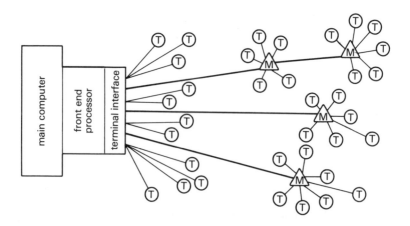

Figure 4.11 **Example of an Asynchronous Terminal Network**

4.6 Summary

The arrangements for connecting asynchronous terminals
to a central computer depend on the level of response
needed, and the cost of providing an acceptable
performance throughout the terminal network. Because of
the PTT's pricing policy for various capacity PSTN
connections, the use of remote multiplexers is usually
advantageous if terminals have to use the PSTN. The
remote multiplexers use high bandwidth connections to
the central computer over the PSTN. Remote terminal
multiplexers can be intelligent in the way they allocate
the bandwidth of a single high speed channel among the
slower terminal channels which they multiplex. Due to
the large amount of processing a central computer
system has to do for a terminal network, many systems
use a small front end processor to do most of the
character processing.

5 Simple Message-based Techniques

Character-based networks are orientated around unintelligent terminals and centralised computer systems. The simple message-based systems covered in this chapter involve more intelligent terminals that are capable of more complex communication, but still involve the use of a central computer system. There are two types of device used mainly on message-based networks, these are 'page mode' VDUs and remote job entry stations. At the end of the chapter there is a brief discussion of distributed computing, which is a natural extension of this type of network.

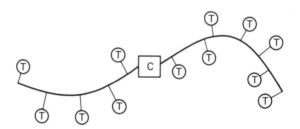

Figure 5.1 **Example of a Multipoint Line Network**

5.1 Multipoint (Multidrop) Lines

The multipoint line network aims to make the optimum use of the transmission medium by having several terminals share the same medium. Figure 5.1 shows an example of a possible network of multipoint lines. Although several multipoint lines may be connected to one central computer, the object of such a line is to connect as many terminals as possible to the one line, thus reducing the cost of the transmission medium. Each terminal requires a terminator; if the PSTN is used then the terminator will be a MODEM. However as only one transmission medium is involved the number of terminators is less than a star network. With one channel, only one message at a time can be transferred, either between a terminal and the computer or the computer and a terminal. To avoid interference strict discipline is needed to control the transmission of messages; this discipline comes from a controller situated at the computer site and is in the form of a polling regime. There are two common polling regimes, hub polling and roll call polling, which are dealt with below. Because the computer has control, messages from the computer to any terminal can be sent as soon as the channel is free. Messages from the terminals require management by polling each terminal to ask if it has a message and then allocating a slot for the transmission of that message. Multipoint schemes may use separate channels for input and output, so that messages from the computer to the terminals can be sent at the same time as the terminals are being polled. The polling is only concerned with input to the computer. As every terminal is attached to the line it receives every message; therefore each message contains an address which every terminal inspects to decide if the message is to be acted on. Each terminal has to wait before information can be sent to the computer, because the terminals buffer the keyboard input into messages. Similarly, as information to a terminal has to wait for the output channel to be free, it is buffered in the computer controller and is output as a message. In this way only messages are exchanged, so the ideal medium is a synchronous character frame channel.

Roll Call Polling

The computer controller polls each terminal individually to ask if the terminal has any data to be sent to the computer. The controller sends a message (see figure 5.2a) which contains the address of a terminal and a command to reply positively if there is information, or negatively if there is no information to be sent. Each terminal inspects every message to see if it contains that terminal's address: if it does the terminal acts on the message. The terminal operator presses the 'send' button when data is ready for sending to the computer, it is then stored in the terminal output buffer. When a polling message is received at the terminal it means that any information stored in the terminal output

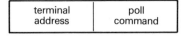

(a) poll message format

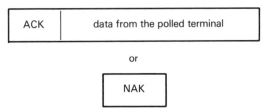

(b) polling reply message formats

Figure 5.2 **Polling Messages**

buffer can be sent to the computer. If there is data in the output buffer a positive reply is sent and this is followed by the data itself. If there is no data a negative reply is returned. Data can only be sent to the computer when a polling message from the computer controller has been received by the terminal.

When a reply has been received from the polled terminal by the computer controller, it will poll the next terminal on its list. If a reply to a polling message is not received within a set time the controller assumes the terminal has been switched off and continues to the next terminal. The list of terminal addresses in the controller determines the sequence of terminal polling. Some controllers are built around a small processor. In these devices the list of terminal addresses can be kept in a small read/write memory area. The main computer can then alter the list to suit the usage of the terminals. If a terminal requires a very quick response compared with another terminal then that terminal's address can occur more than once in the polling list.

Hub Polling

The computer controller in the roll call polling scheme decides which terminal to poll next, and the frequency with which each terminal is polled. In hub polling the terminals on a multipoint line are imagined to be placed on the hub of a wheel. The polling message is then passed from one terminal to the next around the hub. The controller begins the process by sending a polling message to the first terminal in the sequence. That terminal replies either positively, followed by its data in a message, or negatively. At the end of the reply the **terminal** polls the next terminal in the sequence by placing the address of the next terminal and the polling command at the end of its own reply. The next terminal then replies as though it had been polled directly from the controller, and adds a polling message for the next terminal round the hub to its reply. When the last terminal has been polled the controller takes over again.

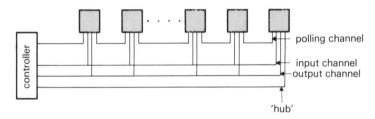

Figure 5.3   **Hub Polling Channels**

The two polling regimes represent the extremes of implementation strategy; compromises can be used to provide the required mix of of facilities. The two regimes can be weighed up by considering the following points.

Response. Roll call polling can provide more flexibility in changing the response which an individual terminal gets from the computer. The response is the interval between polling messages for a particular terminal. Often during the day the required response for terminals can change. By adjusting the poll list in the controller the response can be altered.

Efficiency. Hub polling is more efficient, in terms of work done by the controller. Often a hub polling multipoint line will use three channels; one for messages from the terminal to the computer, one for messages from the computer to the terminal, and one for the polling messages (see figure 5.3). In this scheme the polling message does not need an address as only the next terminal can receive the polling message. Once the controller has begun the poll it can concentrate on sending and receiving information messages. Thus the amount of time used in sending messages not containing data is reduced.

Flexibility. The roll call technique has far more flexibility and responsiveness to failures amongst the terminals. If one of the hub call terminals is switched off the polling cannot continue beyond that terminal to the rest in the sequence. If a hub call terminal is switched off, or breaks down, changes have to be made to the circuit to bypass that terminal, or addresses changed in the preceding terminal.

Hardware. The roll call polling regime requires more work from the controller so it can handle less terminals than a hub call controller, though the actual limit on the number of terminals is more likely to be constrained by line bandwidth. Roll calling also requires more bandwidth for the polling messages which reduces the number of terminals that can be placed on a multipoint line. Hub call terminals need extra logic for adding the polling message and may use an extra channel for the polling message, which will add to the cost of each terminal.

In choosing a particular implementation the designer has to weigh message size and desired response against flexibility and cost before making any decisions.

5.2 Applications

As a multipoint terminal has to store data and transfer
it to the computer, when asked by the computer, such a
terminal is not very useful on an interactive general
purpose timesharing computer. In such a case the user
often requires a response to a single character.   The
transfer of a single data character within a
multicharacter message is not very efficient.   The size
of messages and overheads is discussed later.

   Multipoint terminal networks are very useful where a
'chunk' of information is entered at once, because the
computer does not process the data until it has all been
entered.   Such an application could be entering invoice
details, in a system known as transaction processing.
The format of the invoice is reproduced on the VDU so
the operator has only to enter details such as
addresses, numbers and quantities.   When an invoice has
been completed and the operator is satisfied that it is
correct, the **send** key is pressed so that the next poll
from the computer of that terminal despatches the
information to the computer and a new screen is
formatted.

   An often-mentioned application of multipoint
terminals is in booking airline tickets. All details of
the requested flight are entered, then all the details
such as cost and availability are returned. This whole
system is designed so that a delay, of say 15 seconds,
for the reply is not exceeded very often. A customer
does not like to wait, and it produces a bad image if a
computerised system does not appear to be fast and
efficient. In the case of an airline booking system it
is easy to visualise one set of terminals in the airline
offices for normal enquiries by staff, and another set
in say travel agents for use in answering enquiries
from the public. During working hours most of the data
traffic will come from people working in the offices, so
they would require more polling to meet the response
requirement than the travel agents since most of the
public will be at work. During the lunch hour, or after
work, the VDUs in the offices will not be so busy but
the travel agents will be. The travel agents' VDUs will
need more polling during the lunch hour than the office

VDUs. Though this is a simplified example it does illustrate the need for flexibility and some of the problems a terminal network designer can face.

5.3 Remote Job Entry Stations

The remote job entry (RJE) station is now somewhat dated. An RJE is a small collection of peripherals and a controller to allow users to enter batch jobs, and receive output, at a distance from a central computer (figure 5.4). To a large extent the use of multi-access and remote terminals has reduced the need and usage of a pure RJE. However the idea of having peripherals such as card readers and particularly line printers at sites remote from a computer is becoming more important to support the remote terminal users. Although the RJE is mainly composed of character-based peripherals, the characters are organised into files so that the real basic unit of transfer between the peripheral and the computer is a file. When the transfer is carried out in blocks, RJEs use a message-based synchronous medium in the same way as multipoint lines. It is possible to have an RJE and terminals on a single multipoint line, though a fairly high bandwidth is needed to keep the peripherals busy as well as provide a reasonable response to the terminals.

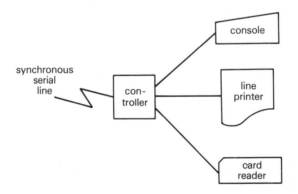

Figure 5.4 **Remote Job Entry (RJE) Station**

The concept of an RJE has been expanded by using a small computer as the controller into a form of distributed computing. Remote job entry stations have a widely used protocol for the exchange of messages; that protocol can also be used for multipoint terminals and is the reason for discussing the two together.

5.4 A Simple Message Protocol

The messages used on multipoint lines and RJE connections are designed to control the exchange of blocks of data characters by embedding control functions within the whole message, the data only being a part of the message. A protocol is very important. It was discussed earlier in the context of character framing techniques and standard character codes. The message protocol most widely used in multipoint and centralised message systems is called Binary Synchronous Communications (BSC). This is a product of IBM, which means that although many other computer manufacturers may support it, they normally prefer to use their own protocols.

The binary synchronous communications protocol defines a mechanism for exchanging control messages so that the transfer of data is accomplished between two autonomous pieces of equipment that only have one communication medium in common. Unfortunately BSC was not defined rigorously enough and several variations exist so only the basic structure is discussed here to give the flavour.

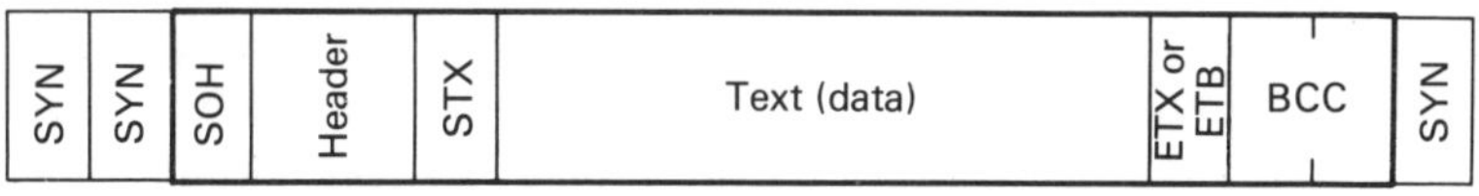

SYN	SYN	SOH	Header	STX	Text (data)	ETX or ETB	BCC	SYN

Figure 5.5 **BSC Message Format**

The outline BSC message format is shown in figure 5.5. The SYN, STX, ETX and ETB are special characters from the character code being used; they are usually called control characters. The control characters are used to delimit the various parts of the message.

SOH This character means that a header is included in the message and all characters up to the next control character are part of the header. The format of the header can vary.

STX This character means that the following characters are the 'text' of the message, or the data. If a header is not included in the message this character will be the first one. The text field must be an exact number of characters. Thus the BSC protocol is best at transferring blocks of characters.

ETX This marks the end of the text of a user message. If there is too much data in a user's message to fit into a single transmission block, this character means that this is the last transmission block in that message transfer.

ETB This character is used where more data from a message follows in another transmission block. This character marks the end of data in this transmission block.

The BCC is a Block Character Check, it is a check on the message calculated by the sender. Most BCC checks use parity calculated on all the characters in the message, though some versions of BSC do use cyclic redundancy checking. The use of checks in message protocols is covered in chapter 6.

From the format shown in figure 5.5 it can be seen that the text field is only part of the whole block of characters transferred. The header, and BCC, contain the information used by the protocol to transfer the data. The extra characters used by the protocol are redundant to the information being transferred; this redundancy reduces the efficiency of the data channel. All protocols introduce redundant information: the more complex the protocol the more redundant information is added.

The operation of the BSC requires the sender and receiver to

1. establish connection – the sender must be sure the receiver is ready

2. transfer the data securely – no errors must occur nor must any data be lost

3. terminate the transfer, so that the receiver knows there is no more data.

This sequence of connection, transfer, disconnection will occur again later. To establish a connection in the BSC protocol the sender sends off a message having the single character ENQ in the text field. This means 'I have some data for you'. Assume the sender is the computer and the receiver is an RJE. The receiver gets the ENQ and responds with a message having as its text another special control character, ACK0, which means 'go ahead'. When the computer receives the go-ahead the connection is established; it then sends a block of data in a message. Having sent one message containing data the computer must wait to see if the message has arrived safely. When the RJE receives the data message the BCC is recalculated from the received message and checked against the BCC in the message. If the checksum is correct then the message is assumed to be free from errors and is stored. To tell the computer that the data message has arrived intact, another special message containing the ACK character is returned. If the BCC calculated by the receiver does not match the BCC in the message the receiver assumes that an error has appeared in the message so it discards the whole message. The receiver then sends a message containing a NAK character back to the computer.

When the computer receives an ACK message it knows its last message has been transferred correctly. If there is more data to be sent another data message is made up and is transmitted; the computer then waits again. If there is no more data the computer sends a message containing an EOT character which means the transfer is complete. If the computer receives a NAK

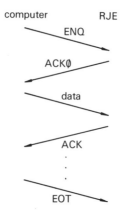

Figure 5.6 **Example BSC Exchange**

message in response to its data message, it sends the
previous data message again. The previous message has
to be stored by the sender in case it is needed. When
an ACK has been received the previous message can be
deleted. A diagram of this transfer is shown in figure
5.6.

Transmitting information using the BSC protocol is
much more complex than just sending characters using an
asynchronous communications medium. This is because
there is usually a human on the terminal at the other
end of an asynchronous line who can tell if data is
missing, or in error, and act appropriately. The need
to check for errors, or lost messages, means a reply is
needed for all messages. If the receiver is too busy to
take a message, or does not have room to store it, it
can ignore the message knowing that the sender will
retransmit it. If a reply to a message is not received
within a certain time (this is called a time out) the
message is sent again. Messages are only repeated so
many times before the sender gives up. If the message
is lost, a time out ensures that the message is
repeated. If the sender times out because the receiver
has gone down the sender will abort the exchange after a
number of retries. In the BSC protocol only one message
is outstanding at any time; this means the transmission

line is idle waiting for the reply. Also, data is only transferred in one direction.

The details of passing blocks of characters, separated by SYN characters, on a synchronous medium should now be clear. Each block of characters is a message consisting of a header, text and check characters. All the protocols in the communication can be viewed as working in layers. At the bottom layer are the electrical signals representing the bits. At the next level are the synchronous characters made up of bits; the characters consist of SYN bit patterns and others. At the next level up is the BSC message; each message is a group of characters separated by SYNs. At the top level is the data, carried in the BSC message which the user eventually sees on the VDU or a line printer. This layered, or hierarchic, approach to communications is extended in later chapters.

From figure 5.6 it can be seen that the transfer of data in one direction involves the transfer of messages back and forth between the sender and receiver. The messages tell each party that the previous part of the transfer was, or was not, satisfactory and to proceed, or to repeat the last message. This exchange of messages is called a handshake. With the concept of a hierarchy they are the major characteristics of computer communications. The purpose of the handshake is to enable both parties to know what the other is doing: absence of any reply messages indicates the other party is not doing anything about the transfer.

At each level in the protocol hierarchy there is a handshake going on. At the lowest level the presence of the electrical signal, or audio signal if a modem is being used, means there is a physical connection. If the signal disappears then transmission is stopped and attempts are made to reconnect the physical link. At the character level the SYN character being received means that the remote end is in synchronisation with the local transmission and ensuring that synchronisation is maintained. At the message level, the various messages such as ENQ, NAK, ACK, EOT, enable the two ends to agree to transfer data, ensure that the data is transferred reasonably securely, and finally complete the transfer neatly.

5.5 Distributed Computing

Early computer systems consisted of centralised processing units, with possible remote job entry stations attached to them. So, for instance, a bank would hold all the information about its customers at a central computer, and the day's transactions would be prepared at each branch and run through an RJE. The manager would then receive information for the next day's work at his branch.

With the arrival of remote access terminals minicomputers were used to control the communications network at the computer, as a front end processor. With a minicomputer handling the communications, more complex protocols could be used. The next step was to use a minicomputer as the controller in the RJE itself. Using a minicomputer at the remote site allowed the following developments.

1. More complex I/O devices could be used.

2. Local storage on tapes and discs.

3. Remote concentration of terminals, using the mini as the concentrator to a small star network.

4. More complex facilities in the transmission of data.

5. Local computing independent of the central computer.

Continuing the banking example, the use of distributed intelligence gives a branch its own small computer on which are kept all the local customer records. The branch computer then communicates with the central computer, sending only a summary of each day's trading which has been prepared as a result of processing the day's work locally.

Eventually the central computer becomes overloaded again, this time because all the communications traffic is centered around it (see figure 5.7). The next logical step is to connect the branches together so they can exchange information directly. This leads to the establishment of a general computer network. When all communication is based on a star network, such as that in figure 5.7, there are no addressing or routing problems. All messages must pass through the central site, and can only go by one route. In a general network a message can go to any other site, usually by at least two possible routes. The techniques required for general computer networks are the subject of chapter 7 onwards.

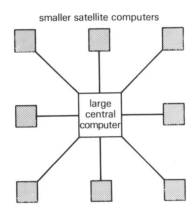

Figure 5.7   **Centralised Computer Network**

The concept of distributed processing covers any situation where a number of processing sites share the load which would previously have been handled by a central computer. The development of distributed processing was achieved by placing general purpose computers (minicomputers) where previously a hardwired controller had been used. The processing power is then used to increase the flexibility and complexity of the equipment. It is now certain that the use of microprocessors will further advance this idea of replacing dedicated hardware by a programmable processor. The use of micro-processors will mean the demand for, and use of, general purpose computer networks will increase dramatically in the future.

British Telecom already provides a Prestel terminal facility so that every home with a suitable TV set can access a huge data base kept on computers. Plans are advanced for the Prestel terminal to be used to program in BASIC and link into other computers.

5.6 Summary

This chapter has been concerned with centralised message communications, for example multipoint terminals and remote job entry stations. The use of the BSC protocol for exchanging messages has been described as an introduction to data communication protocols. The complexity of the message protocol has introduced some of the problems of maintaining reliable, yet efficient, data transfer through a single medium.

6 *Errors, Error and Flow Control*

The purpose of this chapter is primarily to look at the problem of noise and the various solutions to the problem adopted in computer communications. In synchronous transmission the solutions to the noise problem are also used to solve the flow control problem, so these are considered together.

6.1 The Nature of Errors

Errors in computer communications usually occur in the transmission medium between the sending and receiving equipment. The equipment, such as a computer interface, terminal, or RJE, is expected to handle the data internally without error. In normal practice this model holds true. It is certain that the vast majority of errors introduced into data occur in the transmission medium. The major cause of errors is noise in the medium, which is usually due to extra signals in a wire being used to transmit data. The noise is usually electromagnetic interference from electrical devices physically close to the wire. A familiar form of noise is clicking on a telephone line, caused by exchange equipment operating near the circuit. One advantage of fibre optics as a communications medium is that it is not affected by the electromagnetic noise usually found in a man-made environment.

Once noise occurs in a wire the original data signal has the noise signal added to it. The receiving equipment receives the sum of the data and the noise signals from the transmission medium. If the noise signal does not have much power compared with the power of the data signal, then the noise will not affect the data too much and the receiving equipment can correctly interpret the received signal into the original data. When the noise signal becomes very strong it completely changes the data signal so that it becomes impossible to detect what the original data was. Shannon allowed for noise in his equation to calculate channel capacity by using the ratio S/N (see chapter 2). If the noise is very low in power compared to the data signal power then the capacity of the channel is higher than when the noise and data have similar power. Shannon's equation indicates how much data is received, **on average**, in a channel. Obviously if there is a lot of noise then data is lost, thus losing capacity. Shannon's equation uses average values of the data and noise signal power. A problem for computer communications is that the power of the noise varies quite a lot in a short period of time.

In a speech communication the noise may drown out part of the conversation, or only partly obscure it, or may not be noticeable. There are various degrees of interference from noise. In binary digital communication a bit that is in error, due to noise, must have been changed from its original value. For a bit to change the noise must have reached a level such that the receiver interprets the received signal as being of the opposite value to that transmitted. When a bit does not change then there was effectively no noise, so there is a threshold above which noise causes errors and below which noise has no effect. If only one bit in a message changes, then the whole meaning of the message can be changed, for instance changing a bit in a single instruction in the binary image of a program. Normally a sequential group of bits become changed due to a burst of noise; the number of bits changed (or inverted) are then called an error burst. In between the error bits the remainder of the message remains correct. The frequency and length of error bursts will affect the throughput of data on a channel. This is reflected in the S/N ratio.

When noise occurs on the PSTN, two people talking on the telephone recognise that extra signals have appeared in their conversation because the received message does not make any sense to them. This method of error detecting is possible because the information is processed as it is received by the listener, in order to make sense of it. In computer communications the sending and receiving equipment do not know what the data means – it is only a sequence of bits. The receiver cannot tell which bits are corrupted due to noise, because it does not understand the message. This poses a major problem which is set out in two questions that need to be answered to achieve reliable data transfer.

1. How can the receiver know if there are any errors?

2. What can the receiver do to obtain the correct data?

The only certain fact about errors in communications is that they will occur. This is because it would cost far too much to make an error-free channel, even if one were possible. Working from this fact the sender and receiver must attempt to overcome the errors so as to transfer the data reliably. Because the errors occur randomly it is not possible to be 100% certain that any received data is correct without comparing it with the original. If the original data is available there is no point in transmitting it. If the original data is not available it must be transmitted, and therefore **could** be received with errors. Even if data is transmitted twice and comes out the same it is not impossible (but is very unlikely) that the same error exists in both copies! The receiver must obtain the data with the maximum probability that it does not contain any errors, and with the maximum efficiency. There is a trade off between the probability that the received data is correct and the efficiency with which the data is transferred.

6.2 Error Control

There are three methods of error control used in computer communications.

1. Echo checking.

2. Forward Error Correction (FEC).

3. Automatic Repeat Request (ARQ).

Each of these methods relies on using some of the channel capacity available for data to carry redundant information. The redundant information is used to enable the receiver to answer the first question posed in the previous section. Redundant information is added to the data before transmission to help the receiver detect errors, but by adding more information to be transmitted the channel efficiency for carrying the original data is reduced. The concept of a Hamming distance shows why the extra information is needed to detect the errors. Hamming carried out work in error control and he is particularly famous for his technique, called a Hamming code, used in forward error correction.

Hamming Distance

The Hamming distance between two bit patterns is the number of bits that are different in the patterns in respective bit positions. For instance the bit pattern for the ASCII character 'A' has a Hamming distance of 1 from the ASCII character 'C'.

$$A = 01000001$$
$$C = 01000011$$

The last but one bit is different and there is only 1 difference. This means a burst of noise of length 1 bit could change an 'A' into a 'C', or vice versa. The ASCII characters 'A' and 'B' have a Hamming distance of 2.

$$A = 01000001$$
$$B = 01000010$$

The last 2 bits are different. This means a burst of 2 bits is needed to change an 'A' into a 'B'. Because noise bursts tend to be short a burst of length 1 bit is more likely to occur than a burst of length 2 bits. If there is a burst of noise, then an 'A' is more likely to be changed into a 'C' than a 'B'. Hamming realised this and advocated that some bit patterns in a code should not be used, so that all bit patterns (codes) used in transmission have the maximum Hamming distance. If all the bit patterns used in a transmission have a Hamming distance of 2 from each other, then any 1 bit errors will be immediately detected by the receiver because they will produce a bit pattern that is not used. For instance, if the pattern 0110 is used as a transmission code, then the patterns 1110, 0010, 0100,

0111 would not be used as they have a Hamming distance of only 1 from the used code. If the receiver finds one of these patterns then it can assume that the data has an error because it knows that the sender would not transmit such a pattern. Should we decide to insist that all codes use a Hamming distance of 3 then all 2 bit error bursts will be detected as well as all 1 bit bursts. The cost of this protection is that for every pattern that is not used for transmission the information it could represent has to be transferred using more bits from the patterns that can be used.

The only way the receiver can detect transmission errors due to noise is by receiving a bit pattern that cannot have been transmitted. To enable the receiver to notice illegal bit patterns the sender adds extra information to the original data to make the data conform to those patterns the receiver accepts as legal. This extra information is only used for transmission, but uses some of the channel capacity that could otherwise be used for data. Fortunately there are techniques that can reduce the redundancy considerably, whilst still providing a very high probability of error-free transfer.

6.3 Echo Checking

The echo checking technique involves echoing the data back to the sender for checking. If the sender receives back the data that it sent then it assumes the receiver has the correct data. Redundancy occurs because the data is transmitted twice. A full duplex connection is needed, with plenty of spare capacity to allow for each item of data to be transmitted twice. This method is used with asynchronous terminal-to-computer transfers on timesharing systems. When the user types a character on the terminal keyboard the character is sent to the computer; the computer then echoes the character back and it appears on the terminal display or printer. If the returned character does not match the character sent the user will correct it. Echo checking works well on asynchronous terminal lines as there is plenty of spare channel capacity, and an intelligent operator to handle the errors. The computer has very little extra work to do. The echo checking technique is not very suitable for other situations either because it is wasteful of channel capacity, or because the communication is to be automatic.

6.4 Forward Error Correction (FEC)

This technique involves adding extra bits to the data so that the receiver can not only detect that an error has occurred, but can also find which bit(s) have changed and repair the damage. As the data is binary, once an error has been located to a particular bit it only needs inverting to obtain the correct value. FEC techniques pinpoint the position of the bit in error. There are different methods used in FEC to pinpoint the error bits. Many are used to overcome particular types of error burst, for instance long bursts with long periods of no errors, or lots of short bursts in a short time. Hamming's coding method for FEC will be used as an example, to show how it works and to outline its limitations. A good error correcting code that handles most error situations but does not involve a lot of redundancy has yet to be found.

Hamming Code

The Hamming coding method uses check bits placed among the data bits; each check bit covers a number of data bits. If a bit is corrupted by noise the position of the error can be detected by recalculating the check bits. The check bits are placed in the 'power of 2' positions: 1, 2, 4, 8, etc. With 4 data bits 3 check bits are used as below.

Bit position	7	6	5	4	3	2	1
Check bits				C_3		C_2	C_1
Data bits	D_4	D_3	D_2		D_1		

The check bit in position 8 is not used because it does not check any data bits to the right of position 9. The data bits are covered by the check bits whose positions add up to the position of the data bit. D_1 is covered by C_1 and C_2 because C_1 and C_2 are in positions 1 and 2 which add up to 3, the position of D_1. Similarly D_2 is covered by C_3 and C_1 because their positions (1 and 4) add up to 5 the position of D_2. The check bits covering the data bits are shown in table 6.1.

Table 6.1

Data bit D_1	in position	3	is covered by			C_1, C_2
'' ''	D_2 ''	''	5 ''	''	''	C_1, C_3
'' ''	D_3 ''	''	6 ''	''	''	C_2, C_3
'' ''	D_4 ''	''	7 ''	''	''	C_1, C_2, C_3

Note that D_4 is covered by 3 check bits. The protection is provided by calculating the value of the checks bit from the values of the data bits that each one covers. The calculation is a parity check, using even parity. Even parity is such that an even number of ones occurs in the data bits and the check bit combined. This is easily calculated on a computer by the exclusive-or operation on the data bits. To calculate the check bits it is necessary to know which data bits are involved in each check bit. By rearranging table 6.1 table 6.2 is produced.

Table 6.2

$$C_1 = D_1 \Delta D_2 \Delta D_4$$
$$C_2 = D_1 \Delta D_3 \Delta D_4$$
$$C_3 = D_2 \Delta D_3 \Delta D_4$$

The symbol Δ represents the exclusive-or operation. Table 6.2 gives the computation sequence required to calculate the Hamming code for a particular 4 bit data pattern.

Example 6.1

Code the data 0110, using the Hamming coding method, for transmission.

$$D_1 = 0, \ D_2 = 1, \ D_3 = 1, \ D_4 = 0$$

From table 6.2

$$C_1 = 0 \Delta 1 \Delta 0 = 1$$
$$C_2 = 0 \Delta 1 \Delta 0 = 1$$
$$C_3 = 1 \Delta 1 \Delta 0 = 0$$

(note the operation of even parity)

the 7 bit Hamming code is made up as

D_4	D_3	D_2	C_3	D_1	C_2	C_1
0	1	1	0	0	1	1

giving 0110011 as the 7 bit code which is then transmitted.

When the code is received it is checked to see if there have been any errors. There are two ways this might be done

1. recalculate the check bits

2. look the code up in a table, if there are not too many bits.

As an example to explain further the operation of an error correcting code, the calculation will be done. If speed was required then a table lookup would produce the answer much more quickly on a computer. Of course the Hamming code calculations are also easily implemented in dedicated hardware within the communications interface.

Example 6.2

The pattern 0100011 has been received. Check it for errors and produce the correct data. The respective data and check bits are

D_4	D_3	D_2	C_3	D_1	C_2	C_1
0	1	0	0	0	1	1

Recalculate the check bits from the data bits and compare the results with the actual check bits received, from table 6.2.

$$C_1 = 0 \, \Delta \, 0 \, \Delta \, 0 \quad = 0 \quad \text{received } C_1 = 1$$
$$C_2 = 0 \, \Delta \, 1 \, \Delta \, 0 \quad = 1 \quad \text{received } C_2 = 1$$
$$C_3 = 0 \, \Delta \, 1 \, \Delta \, 0 \quad = 1 \quad \text{received } C_3 = 0$$

It appears that C_1 and C_3 were not received correctly, but of course any bit (or bits) could be in error. The data bits that C_1 and C_3 cover together are D_2 and D_4, but if D_4 was in error C_2 would not be correct either, so it must be D_2 in position 5. Note that the bit positions of C_1 and C_3 add up to 5. Correcting bit 5 by inverting gives the correct data as 0110; compare the corrected received code with the result of example 6.1.

With the Hamming code the position of the bit in error can be determined very quickly by the check bits which appear to be wrong, this is shown in table 6.3.

Table 6.3

Incorrect check bits	Error bit position
C_1	1
C_2	2
C_1 and C_2	3
C_3	4
C_3 and C_1	5
C_3 and C_2	6
C_3 and C_2 and C_1	7

This looks very impressive until it is realised that the Hamming code works if only 1 bit is in error, if 2 bits out of the 7 change due to noise they produce an incorrect result. The Hamming code used in the examples produces the correct data at the receiver with a probability equal to the probability that an error burst will only affect 1 bit in any 7.

The Hamming coding technique is a simple forward error correcting code, but its power is representative of the class of FEC techniques. To calculate the efficiency of the Hamming code consider that for a 7 bit code there are 128 possible patterns of which only 16 are used. The redundancy in terms of bits transmitted, or channel capacity used for data, is 4 data bits for every 7 transmitted which is 57%. To be able to detect, and correct, more than 1 bit in error more redundancy is needed, which further reduces the efficiency.

Despite its low efficiency, forward error correction does have advantages. If a simplex connection is being used then neither echo checking nor automatic repeat request can be considered, as they both require at least a half duplex connection. On some communication systems involving long distances, such as satellite-based communications, the delay in requesting a repeat transmission is so long that FEC may be more economical. If the noise characteristics of a channel are known then complex FEC mechanisms can be used to increase the efficiency at the cost of not being so reliable when the noise patterns deviate from the expected characteristics.

6.5 Automatic Repeat Request (ARQ)

Because most synchronous computer communications uses relatively error-free channels, and the data is usually transferred in blocks, or messages, ARQ techniques are the most widely used. The automatic repeat request technique involves the receiver checking the received bit pattern against a precalculated check from the sender. The sender performs some computation on the data, similar to the parity check in the Hamming code, and adds the result to the end of the data. These extra bits are also called check bits and are usually of fixed length regardless of the size of the data part of the message. When the data is received the receiver repeats the calculation. The assumption is then made that if the data is error free the receiver's calculation should produce the same result as that added to the end of the message by the sender. If the checks do not match, then an error is assumed to have occurred, either in the data or in the received check bits, or both. When an error is found like this the whole message is thrown away, because the check bits do not indicate where the error is, only that there is an error. The sender is then asked to repeat the message containing the error.

By discarding the whole message ARQ techniques would appear to work best on the smallest possible message or block size. However, efficiency on the channel requires the largest possible ratio of data to check bits and message overhead which would require the largest possible message or block size. These two requirements produce a compromise on the block size that can also be affected by the available storage at the receiver and sender. In the above discussion block and message have been used to mean the single unit of transfer on which the check bits are calculated. In some communication systems each unit is a separate message, in other systems the messages are so large that they have to be transmitted as a number of blocks. A message is a complete unit of user's data – it is a logical entity; a block is a physical unit. Confusion can occur when the logical and physical unit coincide.

ARQ uses check bits which are calculated on the data in the block, the check bits are then added to the end of the data and transmitted. The recalculation of the check bits and their comparison them with the received check bits is similar to FEC, but the ARQ technique does not need to pinpoint the bits in error, so less bits are used for checking. Normally 8 or 16 check bits are used for a single block containing up to 2000 data bits. The confidence with which the receiver can declare the data to be free of errors is never 100%, but it can be very close depending on the algorithm used to calculate the check bits.

Polynomial Codes

The most effective checking algorithm currently available involves the use of polynomial codes. These are a recent development, where mathematics has provided a very powerful technique which can be economically used on digital computers. Using a simulation on a block of 260 bits, an improvement of 50 000 was found over parity checking techniques, such as those used in the Hamming code. The effectiveness of the polynomial codes relies on an extensive theoretical treatment of polynomials. Here we are only concerned with how to use them.

The message, or block, consisting of binary bits, is treated as a general polynomial where the bits are the coefficients of the polynomial terms. For instance,

$$10101 = 1x^4 + 0x^3 + 1x^2 + 0x^1 + 1x^0$$
$$= x^4 + x^2 + 1$$

So

$$x^{16} + x^{12} + x^5 + 1 = 10001000000100001$$

Call the message to be transmitted M(x), a polynomial in x. A generating polynomial G(x) is used to calculate the check bits by dividing M(x) by G(x). So we get

$$\frac{M(x)}{G(x)} = D(x) + R(x)$$

Where $D(x)$ is the result and $R(x)$ is the remainder. $R(x)$ is a smaller value than $G(x)$ and in particular will be represented by no more bits than those needed for $G(x)$. Unfortunately this calculation leaves $M(x)$ in a mess. It has to be reconstituted by multiplication. To overcome this $M(x)$ is multiplied by x^n where n is the degree (highest exponent of x) of $G(x)$. The degree of $x^{16} + x^{12} + x^5 + 1$ is 16, so if this is our generating polynomial, $M(x)$ is multiplied by x^{16}.
This gives

$$\frac{M(x).x^n}{G(x)} = M(x) + R(x)$$

$G(x)$ now divides $M(x).x^n$ exactly by $M(x)$, leaving a remainder $R(x)$.

Performing division and multiplication on a digital computer is usually very time consuming. Fortunately binary numbers have some interesting properties when the arithmetic is performed modulo 2. In modulo 2 arithmetic there are no carries from one digit position to the next, so each bit can be operated on separately. A modulo 2 binary division is performed using a shift register and some exclusive-or gates. The calculation of $M(x).x^n$ divided by $G(x)$ can be done very quickly in hardware by using modulo 2 arithmetic. Multiplying $M(x)$ by x^n means shifting $M(x)$ left by n bits.

Polynomial codes are able to detect the following types of errors

1. all odd numbers of bits in error,

2. all error bursts with a length less than the size of the remainder (usually 16 bits),

3. all error bursts longer than the remainder that are not exact multiples of the generator polynomial.

The polynomial $x^{16} + x^{12} + x^5 + 1$ has been chosen as the international standard after much theoretical work and simulation. Other polynomials are also used, of course, but all have similarly high error detection rates.

Some older error checking methods, such as block parity, may still be used in some simple protocols; these techniques have been well explained in other texts such as the book by Barber and Davies. The superiority of polynomial codes, and their adoption by the CCITT ensures that they are the most widely used technique.

The ARQ method of error handling does not just involve the detection of errors, but also the retransmission of blocks found to contain errors. As each block of data is received the check is calculated and compared. If the block is found to contain errors the receiver discards it. Obviously just throwing the received data away does not magically cause the correct data to be retransmitted: the receiver has to inform the sender whether retransmission is needed or not. The receiver and sender have to communicate about the transfer of the data. The format of that communication is a protocol. The simple protocol, BSC, introduced in chapter five enables blocks of data to be transferred reliably. The receiver gives the sender an acknowledgement for each data block; if any are in error a special negative acknowledgement is given. This is similar to a listener nodding his head so that a speaker can see that he is being understood during a conversation. A number of ARQ strategies are used in the handling of transmission and retransmission of messages.

Idle RQ

This is the simplest variation. It is used in the BSC protocol with a minor addition of a binary sequence number. The sender transmits a single data block and then waits for an acknowledgement. The receiver checks the data block, and if it is intact (no errors) a positive acknowledgement is sent back. If an error is detected the block is discarded and a negative acknowledgement is returned. If the block is lost, or its format is destroyed by some control bits being corrupted, no acknowledgement is returned. At the sender, if a positive acknowledgement is received the next block in the transfer is sent; if a negative acknowledgement is received the previous block is retransmitted. The last block transmitted is always

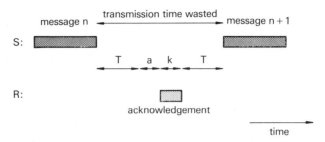

Figure 6.1 **Idle RQ Timing**

kept by the sender, ready for retransmission. If the
sender does not receive an acknowledgement within a
specified time after a block has been transmitted a time
out occurs. The block will normally be retransmitted
after a time out; if a number of time outs occur
successively the sender will assume the receiver is
unable to continue and will abort the transfer. If the
receiver is particularly slow in returning an
acknowledgement it is possible for a time out to occur
before the acknowledgement is received by the sender.
In this case the receiver will have a duplicate copy of
the previous block. To be able to detect duplicates
each data block is given a unique sequence number. The
full use of sequence numbering is taken up later in
section 6.6 on Sequence Numbering and Acknowledgement.

The Idle RQ exchange sequence is shown in figure 6.1
where the sender is S and the receiver R. Idle RQ has
only one outstanding block so the sender does not need
storage for more than the maximum block size. The
receiver always gets the information in sequence as only
one block is transferred at a time. The receiver only
needs to store one block whilst it is checked before it
is passed on to the user. Unfortunately Idle RQ does
not make very efficient use of the communications
medium. If the transmission delay from sender to
receiver is T seconds, and the processing time by the
receiver is k seconds then the sender must wait $2T + k$
seconds before it receives an acknowledgement. The
transmission delay is the time taken for a signal to
travel from the sender to the receiver and includes all
the buffering and hardware delays. The acknowledgement
will take a further a seconds to be transmitted (or

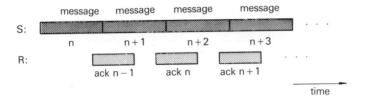

Figure 6.2 **Continuous RQ Timing**

received), so the elapsed time after completing the
transmission of one data block and beginning
transmission of the next is $2T+k+a$ seconds. During
the delay the transmission channel from sender to
receiver is Idle, hence the name Idle RQ. As the
communications channel is usually the slowest part of a
communications system, any inefficiency in its use
affects the performance of the whole system. Where the
value of $2T+k+a$ is very small compared with the
transmission time of a data block the loss of
efficiency is small, but on wideband or long distance
connections the use of Idle RQ becomes very inefficient
as the block transmission time becomes comparable to the
idle time.

Continuous RQ

A method of increasing efficiency over Idle RQ is
continuous RQ. The data blocks are transmitted
continuously so that ideally there is no idle time on
the transmission channel. A number of data blocks are
transmitted in sequence by the sender without waiting
for an acknowledgement. As they arrive at the receiver
they are processed and acknowledged as in Idle RQ. By
the time the sender gets an acknowledgement it will have
transmitted a number of further data blocks, so the
received acknowledgments will lag behind the data
transmissions. Figure 6.2 is a timing diagram showing
the continuous RQ technique. Continuous transmission
without waiting for an acknowledgement of the preceding
block presents some further problems. At the sender
each block transmitted but not acknowledged needs to be
stored in case retransmission is needed. At the
receiver, if a block is found to be in error then a
number of later data blocks will be received before the
block in error can be retransmitted, which may upset the

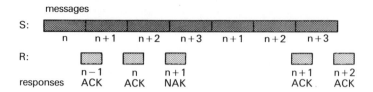

Figure 6.3   **Go–Back–N Example**

sequencing of the data. In case any blocks, data or
acknowledgement, are lost each data block is given a
unique sequence number and the acknowledgement for each
data block uses that sequence number to indicate which
block it is an acknowledgement for. Figure 6.2 shows
the sequence numbers $n-1$, n, $n+1$, $n+2$, etc.
Continuous RQ is important where there is a large value
of T, such as in systems using satellites.

With all protocols the complications arise when an
error occurs. In the ARQ protocol there are two schemes
for handling retransmission when an error occurs.

1. **Go–Back–N**

   When an error occurs, the receiver sends a negative
   acknowledgement indicating that the block of that
   sequence number should be retransmitted. The sender
   retransmits that block, then continues with
   successive blocks even though they may have already
   been transmitted. Figure 6.3 shows block n
   positively acknowledged, but block $n+1$ in error and
   negatively acknowledged. Because of the delay time
   $(2T+k+a)$ the sender has already sent blocks $n+2$
   and $n+3$ before the negative acknowledgement for
   $n+1$ is processed. The receiver ignores blocks
   $n+2$, $n+3$ as they are out of sequence and waits for
   block $n+1$ to arrive. When block $n+1$ has been
   transmitted the sender continues with block $n+2$,
   $n+3$, etc.

2. **Selective Retransmission**

   When the sender receives a negative acknowledgement
   for block $n+1$ it only retransmits block $n+1$. The
   receiver accepts blocks $n+2$ and $n+3$ even though
   block $n+1$ has not been received correctly so they

are out of sequence. After retransmitting block
n + 1 the sender continues with block n + 4, n + 5,
etc. This is shown in figure 6.4.

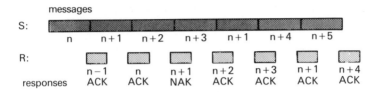

Figure 6.4   **Selective Retransmission Example**

With the Go-Back-N method some blocks are
unnecessarily retransmitted which wastes channel
capacity, whereas with selective retransmission the
receiver has to store later data blocks while waiting
for a retransmission so that the proper sequence of the
data can be maintained. The amount of wasted capacity
in Go-Back-N will depend on how often blocks are
received in error and the number of blocks outstanding
between transmission and acknowledgement. Selective
retransmission makes the most efficient use of the
channel, but requires extra storage at the receiver to
buffer data blocks received out of sequence. The amount
of extra storage again depends on the error rate and the
delays. These two techniques enable a trade off between
channel utilisation and storage requirement at the
receiver. As the storage at the receiver will always be
of fixed size, most protocols use the Go-Back-N method
to ensure that the storage limitation does not cause
serious problems in worse case conditions.

6.6 Sequence Numbering and Acknowledgement

A communication system is designed so that a stream of
data is fed in at one end and a copy of that stream is
produced at a remote site. The probability of the
received data being a correct copy is a function of the
error detecting method being used. The maintenance of
the correct sequence of the data is a function of the
flow control mechanism in the protocol. Earlier in the

chapter the problem of duplicate message blocks was introduced.

The use of blocks to transmit larger pieces of information, such as a file, presents three problems in ARQ.

1. The receiver must be able to maintain the correct sequence of data in the information unit (for example, a file).

2. Any blocks already transmitted, but not acknowledged, must be stored by the sender in case they have to be retransmitted.

3. The receiver will have a limited amount of memory so it is possible for the sender to transmit faster than the receiver can handle the data.

These three problems introduce what is known as flow control. Techniques for quenching a sender to solve problem (3) are an aspect of communications protocols which is discussed later in chapter 8, within the context of X25.

As flow control and error handling in ARQ-based protocols are combined, it is useful to look at such a technique at this point. The techniques for maintaining sequence and detecting duplicate message blocks are covered here. The example of the combined flow and error control mechanism which will be shown here is based on Go-Back-N ARQ. This is very similar to the mechanism used in X25.

So that the data sequence can be maintained, each block of data transferred across the transmission medium is given a unique sequence number. The sequence numbers are then used to acknowledge the data blocks and control the data flow. Normally in computer communications data is exchanged in both directions so the acknowledgements can be piggy-backed onto data blocks being transmitted in the return direction. The header placed in front of each data block then contains two numbers: the sequence number of this data block, and the sequence number of an acknowledged data block that was transmitted in the opposite direction. This only works for positive acknowledgement of data blocks; when a protocol uses this method it is called a positive acknowledgement protocol. A special message is still needed for negative acknowledgement.

The sequencing is arranged so that each side knows the sequence number of the first data block. This means that the receiver knows the number of the first data block it will receive. Each end keeps two variables: the sequence number of the next data block it will transmit $T(s)$ and the sequence number of the next data block it should receive $R(s)$. These two variables are usually set to zero when the connection is established, which gives the common start value. Consider two computers which are about to transfer data, called computer **A** and computer **B**. The initial value of **A**'s $T(s)$ is 0, the initial value of **B**'s $R(s)$ is 0; thus **A** will begin by sending data block number 0 and **B** will begin by expecting data block number 0: the two computers are synchronised on the sequence numbers. Each transmitted data block will contain two numbers: S which is the sequence number of that data block and is a copy of $T(s)$, and K which is a positive acknowledgement for all data blocks numbered $K-1$ and backwards that have been transferred in the opposite direction. K is a copy of $R(s)$. The acknowledgement number, K, will be easier to understand after the next paragraph.

When **A** sends a data block to **B** it copies $T(s)$ into the S field in the protocol header of the block; it then increments $T(s)$ so that it always contains the sequence number of the next block to be sent. **A** also copies the value of its $R(s)$ variable into the K field in the block header. When **B** receives the data block, and there are no errors, it compares S with its $R(s)$; if they are the same then this is the block that **B** needs to maintain the data sequence. **B** then increments $R(s)$ as it now expects to receive the next data block whose sequence number is one more than the current one. **B** then inspects K, as K is the value of the next block **A** was expecting; $K-1$ is the sequence number of the last block **A** received before

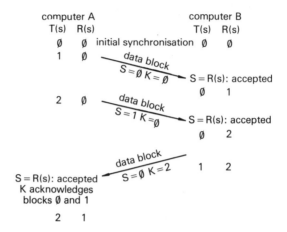

Figure 6.5   Sequence Number Operation

sending this data block. Thus **A** is acknowledging the receipt of the last K−1 blocks from **B**.   Any blocks numbered K−1 and down may now be removed from the retransmission buffers at **B**.   This scheme is shown in figure 6.5 and figure 6.6 shows what happens when an error occurs.

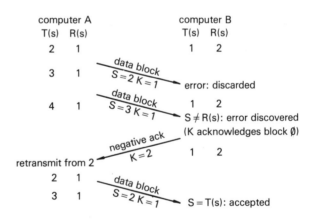

Figure 6.6   Sequence Numbers in Error Recovery

If a very large amount of data is being transmitted, the sequence numbers could become very large and require a large number of bits in each block header.   The sequence numbers used in most protocols are modulo numbers that recycle once they reach a certain value. For instance the X25 protocol, discussed in chapter 8, uses modulo 8 numbers (0, 1, 2, 3, 4, 5, 6, 7, 0, 1, ...) which only need 3 bits for each number in the header. As each data block has to have a unique sequence number so that duplicates can be detected, care has to be taken that new data blocks sent do not have the same sequence number as data blocks not yet acknowledged. To achieve this a window technique is used. The window size is the maximum number of data blocks that can be outstanding (unacknowledged) at any time.

The maximum window size is governed by the sequence number modulo range. The worst case situation occurs when the sender despatches a full window but receives no acknowledgements (due to transmission failure); but the receiver has accepted all of the data. The receiver is now ready for the data following the window. In a selective retransmission scheme with a window of w the sequence number range (modulo number) must be at least $2w+1$. Thus in the worst case, if the sequence number range was less than $2w+1$ some of the retransmissions would be accepted as new data by the receiver. In a Go-Back-N retransmission scheme the sequence number range must be $w+1$ as the receiver will only accept the next data in sequence and ignore the retransmissions of accepted data. In X25, using modulo 8 numbers, the maximum window size is 7.

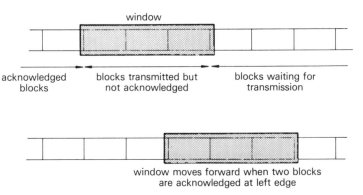

window

acknowledged blocks

blocks transmitted but not acknowledged

blocks waiting for transmission

window moves forward when two blocks are acknowledged at left edge

Figure 6.7   **The Window Mechanism**

Figure 6.7 shows in diagramatic form how a fixed-size window moves across the sequence numbers. As all outstanding data blocks have to be stored by the sender, the window size will govern how much retransmission buffer space is needed by the sender. At the receiver the window size governs how much storage is needed to ensure that all correctly received blocks can be handled efficiently. If the user at the receiving end is not ready, or is not taking data fast enough, the receiver may have to take up to the window size of data blocks before acknowledging any, or discarding any. When the sender receives an acknowledgement for any data blocks, it moves the window forward and transmits new data blocks. Thus the receiver can briefly control the flow of data by delaying acknowledgement, but not for long or the sender will time out and abort the connection. Normally the window size is set by the receiver to indicate the buffer space available for the connection; and as such is an important parameter of flow control.

When an error is detected in a block, the receiver cannot use any information in the block as it cannot tell where the error is, so the whole block is discarded and the next one is awaited. When the next block arrives it does not have the correct sequence number as the block with the sequence number whose value is in R(s) has been discarded. Any data block arriving whose sequence number does not match the value of R(s) means an error has occurred, or a block has been lost. The receiver sends a special negative acknowledgement message containing the value of R(s), which is the sequence number of the error block. When the negative acknowledgement is received by the data sender the appropriate block can be retransmitted. This sequence is shown in figure 6.6, which uses Go-Back-N.

Using a window size which is known at both ends of a connection implies that the sequence numbers of all incoming data blocks must fall within certain boundaries, even if blocks are discarded or lost. The receiver will check the sequence numbers as follows. The block sequence number S must be in the range

$$R(s) - 1 \leq S < R(s) + W \qquad (6.1)$$

where W is the window size. If R(s) = S then no error
has occurred and the data is accepted; if

$$R(s) < S < R(s) + W$$

then an error has occurred and a block has been lost or
discarded. If S = R(s) − 1 then the data block is a
duplicate; this is a special case which can only occur
if the transmitted sequence of data blocks is
maintained; on some computer networks that may not be
so. If S is outside the range given in 6.1 above then a
sequence number error has occurred and the two ends have
become   unsynchronised.   The   protocol   must   have   a
mechanism for recovering from this error, such as a
reset.   The acknowledgement number K must be in the
range

$$T(s) > K \geq T(s) - W \qquad\qquad (6.2)$$

If K is outside this range then it acknowledges a block
that is not in the retransmission buffer, and is
therefore not outstanding! If such an error is found the
two ends have become unsynchronised.

In some computer networks where the packet sequence
is not maintained, or packets may be lost, or delayed,
the above sequence number errors should be ignored as
they are a characteristic of the transport medium.
Normally the protocol using the sequence numbers will
take account of the nature of the network and act
accordingly.

The above mechanism of sequence numbers, send and
receive variables gives a very efficient sequencing and
acknowledging   method   where   only   negative
acknowledgements need special messages.   The positive
acknowledgements are piggy-backed in data blocks going
in the reverse direction.   Normally such a scheme is
used in a continuous RQ system with Go-Back-N. Sequence
numbering with modulo 2 numbers is used in Idle RQ to
detect missing and duplicate data blocks.   This
discussion of sequencing and acknowledging has used the
idea of each data block having a sequence number, the
implication being that a data block is the same as a
block in the BSC protocol, or synchronous transmission
block. This is the case in some protocols, such as X25

or BSC, but not in all. In at least one network protocol a 'data block' is an 8 bit byte for which 32 bit sequence numbers are used. Each message sent contains a number of blocks: the message header contains the sequence number of the first 8 bit byte in the message. The size of the data block is immaterial to the previous discussion which holds for all data block sizes.

6.7 Summary

The nature of noise in data communications is such that it produces bursts of errors. The special problem for computer communications is detecting the presence of errors with a high probability of success, and then correcting them. In order to detect errors redundant information has to be added to the data that is to be transmitted. Two methods of detecting and correcting errors are Forward Error Correction and Automatic Repeat Request. In FEC a large amount of redundant information is used to detect the error and pinpoint the bits that are in error so they can be corrected by the receiver. In ARQ a small number of redundant bits are used to detect errors in a piece of transmitted data; when an error is detected the sender is asked to repeat the transmission.

As ARQ is the most widely used technique in computer communications it has been covered in some detail, particularly the use of sequence numbers in a combined error and flow control mechanism.

7   *Computer Network Technology*

The communications techniques covered so far have been concerned with centralised systems. Terminal networks are all built around a central computer; similarly remote job entry stations are usually connected to a single computer. In the remaining chapters some of the problems and techniques of a network of intercommunicating devices are discussed. The devices at present connected to networks are usually general purpose computers, with their own terminal networks. One reason for networking multi-access computers, rather than terminals or smaller devices, is that these computer systems already existed when networking was proposed. A second reason is that the protocols used in computer networks are very complex so that only a large computer system would have sufficient spare computing power to implement them. However terminals can be directly attached to a network, as will be shown in chapter 9. In the near future computer networks will become as widespread as the telephone network, and large scale integration will enable cheap processors to handle the protocols. The result will be the networking of every sort of computing device.

This chapter is primarily concerned with the technology used to connect the computers and devices that make up a computer network. For the purposes of description the range of technology has been divided into three areas

wide area networks
radio and satellite broadcast networks
local (or private) networks

The network technology includes the techniques used to interconnect the computing devices and physically transfer information from one computing device to another.

7.1 Wide Area Networks

The term 'wide area network' is applied to a network that covers a large physical area, say a whole country or large area under one administration. Such an area may be world wide where a multinational organisation owns the network. The basic communication media used are dedicated circuits, usually of about 50 kHz bandwidth. Where digital circuits are available the bandwidth would be 64 kHz. Examples of such networks are PSS, ARPAnet, TYMNET, TELENET, etc; details of some of these networks are given at the end of this section. For reasons explained in chapter 3, the physical circuits are usually provided by a PTT, although in the case of PSS the whole network is also run by the PTT.

Although 50 kHz bandwidth seems to be a lot compared with the 3 kHz nominal bandwidth of the voice telephone line, it is not very much when high speed or large volume transfers of information are required. Even at these high speeds the channel capacity is a resource that needs to be used efficiently.

It is now necessary to see how information can be transferred from one computer to any other on the network. (In this context 'computer' means any computing device capable of sending or receiving information from the network.) The problem falls into two parts. The first is that of transferring information via a medium, such as a wire, and has been covered in chapters 2 and 3. The second part is concerned with addressing and routing. If there were only two computers on a network, then they could be connected by two channels, one for each direction, and whatever one computer transmitted the other would be bound to receive. When more computers are added, the bi-directional connection solution can be extended by having each computer connected to every other computer by a bi-directional connection. To send a message to a particular computer the appropriate connection is selected (addressed); thus the routing of a message is carried out by the sender. Using a dedicated connection between every computer on the network is very expensive. If there are n computers on the network then $(1/2)n(n-1)$ lines are needed, and have to be paid for!

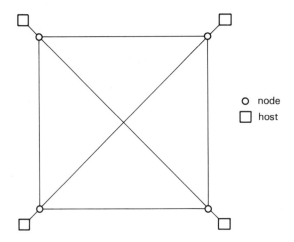

Figure 7.1 **Fully Connected Network**

Figure 7.1 shows a fully connected network with four
computers and six connections. As a single computer
would not normally be communicating with every other
computer on the network at the same time, most of the
lines would be unused in a fully connected network.
Therefore to increase the utilisation of the connection
circuits, their number is reduced, and switching is
introduced within the network.

   There are three forms of switching that can be used
in communications

                       circuit switching
                       message switching
                       packet switching.

Circuit Switching

Circuit switching is used on the PSTN to connect
telephone subscribers. To use it for a computer network
each computer would have a private circuit to a local
exchange, and the exchanges would be connected to form a
network.

   Whenever two computers wish to exchange information,
a physical (electrical) path is established between them
via the exchanges. The path is then disconnected when
the connection is closed. The circuit has been

'switched' by the exchanges. This method of connection
is not used on established computer networks. The major
disadvantages of circuit switching are

1. The cost of the equipment is very high, whereas the
   resulting circuit is not necessarily of high enough
   quality for computer communications.

2. The resulting circuit can only be used by the two
   computers on the call, thus the equipment is
   dedicated to the circuit. In particular the
   connection from the computer to the exchange is
   dedicated. To enable a single computer to
   communicate with more than one other computer at the
   same time extra equipment is needed for each
   simultaneous call. If there are no connections all
   the equipment is idle but being payed for.

3. The time taken to set up the physical path can be
   very long in computer terms (often several seconds).

As high speed connection using good quality circuits is
important for efficient computer networks, circuit
switching is discounted in favour of the other methods.
Circuit switching is used for some networks connecting
computers; for instance the Nordic Data Network.

   Circuit switching has two advantages

1. Charges are made only for the time that a call is
   connected. If infrequent and short connections are
   all that is required, then circuit switching may be
   advantageous to the customer. It is expected that
   many slower devices, such as terminals, will be
   connected to national computer networks via the PSTN
   to gain this advantage.

2. Where a single device is used for long periods, such
   as a facsimilie machine, circuit switching is
   economically advantageous. This is particularly
   true where digital facilities, such as X21, are
   available.

Message Switching

To overcome problems in setting up and taking down physical circuits via exchanges, computer networks use permanent circuits and switch the data. A partially connected network is used in which each computer has a permanent circuit to a number of its neighbours, but not to all computers on the network. An example will illustrate the basic operation of 'information switching' where the unit of information is a message.

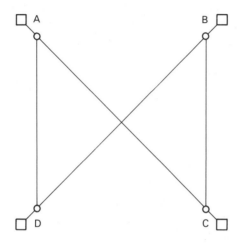

Figure 7.2   **Partially Connected Network**

In figure 7.2, if the computer at **A** wishes to send a message to **B**, the message must pass through either **D** or **C**. The points on the network are called nodes. **A** will address the message to **B** by placing the address of **B** in the message header. The message and address are then sent on the circuit to **D**. At **D** the node inspects the address; if the address is '**D**' the message is given to the computer; if the address is not '**D**' the message is forwarded on a circuit that the node believes will enable the message to be delivered. In this case **D** will forward the message to **B**. Thus the node at **D** has switched the message onto the appropriate output circuit. In this example two major characteristics of a computer network can be seen.

1. Addressing
   The message is addressed to a remote destination and
   sent on the next stage of its route.

2. Store and Forward
   Each message is received into the node storage so
   that it can be processed as a whole unit. Usually
   an error check is carried out (see chapter 6) and
   the whole message has to be received before this can
   be completed. The message is then inspected for
   routing information so that the node can decide
   which output circuit to use to forward the message.

   The nodes have been introduced in the network to
carry out the functions of routing and store and forward
so the host computer is separated from the network
operation as much as possible. The 'hosts' are the user
computers which wish to use the network. Often a number
of hosts will be attached to a single node.

   The node computers are usually minicomputers chosen
for their ability to respond in real time to the
communications devices. Each node receives incoming
messages and stores them. When a complete message has
been received the destination address is inspected so
that the message can be placed on the output queue of a
circuit to forward the message. If the message is for a
host attached to the node the output circuit will be the
one connected to the host. If the message is for a
distant host (on another node) the node must forward the
message to another node on the route to the distant
host. While the message is in the node store, waiting
to be processed or waiting for output, it is, of course,
being delayed. How a node actually goes about routing
is briefly discussed in chapter 10.

   The connection into any one node may be used to carry
messages from several different computers, as may the
connection between the node and host, so the physical
equipment involved is used more efficiently than in
circuit switching. This multiplexing of messages is the
most important advantage of message and packet switching
computer networks.

To distinguish between message and packet switching it is necessary to understand what a message is. This has already been introduced in earlier chapters, but a more detailed discussion is given here. The easiest way of defining a message is to say that it is a unit of information which is exchanged by users of a network. This means the characteristics of a message are only dependent upon the user or the application. A message could be a few bits (say an enquiry into a data base) or a file, or even a whole data base. In a message switching network the whole message is passed from one node to another as a complete entity. Compared with circuit switching, a message switching network has the following characteristics.

1. Any computer (or node) can communicate with any other computer without having a direct physical connection.

2. Any computer can communicate with several others using the same equipment by multiplexing messages.

3. There is no delay due to circuit set up, but messages are delayed when they pass through a node en route.

The messages can be transferred between nodes, and nodes and hosts, using an ARQ protocol (see chapter 6).

Characteristic 3 implies that there is no delay due to the use of a network other than the store and forward operation of the nodes. This is true in some networks using pure datagram techniques. However in most networks the internode protocol used within the network introduces some delays. Any network using a virtual circuit protocol, at any level, will introduce a delay when the message, or packet is given to the network. In many networks the local node negotiates for resources within the network before actually forwarding a message. This is true of an X25 network when the call is first set up, and is true of every message on the ARPA network.

A user of a message switching network will pass the network a message, together with a destination address, and the user will receive messages as single units.

Advantages and Disadvantages

The advantages of message switching, over circuit switching are

1. The sender may dispatch the message when convenient, even if the receiver is not ready, as the network will store the message for delivery. However if network resources (such as storage) run out, an undelivered message may be deleted and thus lost; this depends on the network protocols.

2. Computers can exchange information at different speeds, as the network will buffer the message.

3. Broadcasting of a message may be possible.

4. Equipment is used more efficiently.

5. Messages may be handled by priority.

Each message is treated as a single unit. However, there are also some disadvantages.

1. A very long message will hold up other, perhaps more urgent, messages as it monopolises a circuit for the duration of its transmission.

2. As a message may be very large, the node computer may not have enough memory to store it before forwarding it; in this case the message is lost.

3. A very large message may monopolise the storage of a node, because it cannot be delivered, so that other messages cannot be received by this node.

Packet Switching

The disadvantages of message switching relate to the possible occurrence of 'large' messages, where the exact value of large will depend on the network. If a network could be certain of only handling 'small' messages, the disadvantages would disappear. The transfer of messages is a user requirement, so a network that meets user needs must be able to handle very large messages as well as small messages. The solution to these two conflicting requirements is to break the user's message into small **packets** for transfer through the network and have the packets reassembled into the message by the receiver. Figure 7.3 shows how a message can be broken into packets. Note that the message header is included as the data in the first packet and that each packet has its own header. This refinement produces packet switching, which is the most widely used switching technique for computer networks.

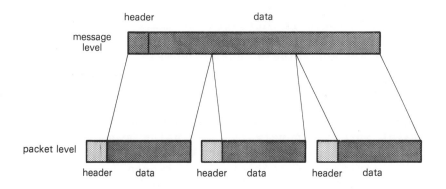

Figure 7.3   **Message Broken into Packets**

The physical organisation of a packet switching network is the same as for message switching. The network is a partially connected mesh of nodes. For practical reasons most networks use special node computers to perform the switching, with the user computers being attached to the nodes. On the ARPA network in the United States the nodes are called Interface Message Processors (IMPs) because they take messages from the user computers (known as hosts) and

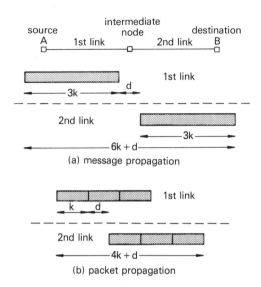

Figure 7.4 **Message Transfer vs Packet Propagation**

break them into packets. The receiving IMP will reassemble the message and give it to the destination host. ARPA network messages do have a maximum size limit. The term host (which originated from the ARPA network) is now widely used to mean a user computer system attached to a network. Figure 7.2 shows a partially connected network with hosts and nodes. The nodes are part of the network, so the hosts use a well defined interface for accessing the node to enable data transfer across the network. By using a node separated from the host, all of the packet switching functions, such as storage and routing, are removed from the host. However the host still needs considerable software to handle the protocols used to access the node and to transfer data to other computers on the network. Chapter 8 discusses a protocol used to access a node from a host and chapter 9 discusses host-to-host protocols.

The advantages that packet switching has over message switching are

1. The small maximum packet size makes storage allocation and management easier in the switching nodes, sufficiently so for minicomputers to be used.

2. The multiplexing of packets enables several messages to be interleaved on one circuit, reducing the delay seen by the user.

3. The total transmission time (delay) through the network is reduced. Figure 7.4(a) shows a message passing from **A** to **B** which would normally require $6k + d$ seconds to reach B, where $3k$ is the transmission time of the whole message on one link and **d** is the node delay. If the message is broken into three packets, each taking **k** seconds to transmit (figure 7.4b), the whole message arrives at B in $4k + d$ seconds. The difference increases with the number of links traversed and the size of the message.

It would appear that packet switching solves all the problems of wide area network organisation: it uses fixed high speed lines and minicomputers for nodes; it is also more efficient and responsive than message switching. However, although packet switching is a better technique with which to implement a computer network, users still want to transfer messages. Packet switching introduces another layer of complexity and translation between the user and the physical network transporting the bits. Fortunately, the cost of processing is falling so the extra cost is outweighed by the practical advantages. A second cost, not so easily overcome, is that each packet will have its own overheads (bits used by the various protocols) as well as those used by each message; this will reduce the efficiency of the physical circuits.

The conclusion drawn from consideration of these three switching techniques is that packet switching, especially used in a partially connected mesh of nodes with wideband circuits, is currently the best technique for wide area computer networks. Packet switching is also used in other network technologies, rather than message switching, for the same reasons.

Examples of Wide Area Networks

Wide area networks have been in existence since the early 1970s. The best known example is the ARPA network in the United States. This network was established by a government research agency (Advanced Research Projects Agency) to link together computer centres that had contracts for government (and in particular defence) research so that research workers could share the available computing resources. The network itself also forms part of a research project to evaluate the feasibility of a large computer network, and to investigate techniques that could be used in such a network.

The ARPA network has been very successful in showing that the concept of resource sharing by use of a network is feasible. One of the most noticeable advantages that the network has introduced is a mail facility. This allows each user with access to a computer on the network to exchange mail with all the other network users. The mail facility is probably one of the main sources of traffic on the ARPA network and has certainly improved the amount of communication between researchers at different sites.

The basic techniques used within the ARPA network have been influenced by the defence aspects of the research, particularly the need for a fast response and resilience to the failure of any part. The network consists of a mesh of partially connected nodes called Interface Message Processors (IMPs). Each IMP can have up to four hosts connected to it and may be connected to up to four other IMPs. Each IMP accepts messages from the hosts of up to 8K bits in length (1K = 1024). The IMP breaks the message into 1K bit packets which are then forwarded through the network of IMPs to the IMP attached to the destination host. This destination IMP reassembles the message before delivering it to the destination host. If a host wishes to send a message of more than 8K bits it must break the message up itself, into 8K packets, and the destination host must reassemble the message from the 8K packets. Thus the translation between messages and packets takes place at two levels. Within the network of IMPs, packets (1K) are sent individually along whichever route is best at the time, so that packets in a single message may use different routes and may arrive at the destination IMP out of sequence. The destination IMP has to reassemble the message from the packets as they arrive. However, messages passed from the host to the IMP are delivered in the same sequence to the destination host. An example of one of the ARPA network host-to-host protocols is given in chapter 9.

The British Telecom network PSS (Packet Switching Service) is an example of a new network provided by a PTT as a public service. The design requirements for such a network are different from those of the ARPA network so they have resulted in a network with different characteristics. The network topology consists of a number of **exchanges** which are also partially connected. Each exchange is connected to a number of host computers in its area. The exchanges contain the node computers, the number of node computers in each exchange depending on the number of hosts attached to the exchange. The hosts use an access protocol called X25 to enable them to make virtual calls to other hosts. A host will give the local exchange the destination address of the host with which it wishes to communicate. The network will route the call to the destination exchange which will then complete the call to the destination host. The call is represented by information kept at all the exchanges on the route. The information is then used to forward the packets transferred on the call. Once the call has been established the hosts may exchange their own information. This is very similar to circuit switching on the PSTN although it is provided using packet switching techniques. The PSS network techniques are different from those on the ARPA network, where each message is addressed and transferred separately. The hosts can use a single link to the PSS exchange to carry a number of virtual calls to other hosts, thus the link is used to multiplex the calls. The X25 protocol is covered in detail in chapter 8.

7.2 Radio and Satellite Broadcast Networks

These networks differ from wide area networks in the way
in which the channel is used for communication between
users. Broadcast networks use a channel to which all
the users are connected, so all the users receive any
transmission made on the channel. At present the two
types of channel in use are local radio, covering up to
a few hundred kilometres, and satellite channels which
are used to span very large distances. Other types of
broadcast channel that may be used are a twisted pair of
wires (often abreviated to 'twisted pair'), a length of
coaxial cable, and an optical fibre; these are discussed
in the next section on local networks.

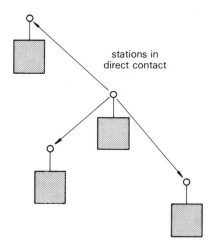

stations in
direct contact

Figure 7.5   **Broadcast Radio Network Topology**

   Networks using radio and satellite channels have
special problems because noise in the channel can cause
errors. There is also the problem of allocating the
channel for transmission. The first operational
broadcast computer network was built at the University
of Hawaii using local radio transmission and many of the
techniques and much of the terminology derive from this
first network. The paper by R. Khan (listed in the
bibliography) contains more details of packet radio
techniques.

Every node receives all packets transmitted on the broadcast channel. When the received packet is complete, the node checks the packet for errors and then checks the destination address. If the address of the receiver matches the packet destination address, it is accepted; otherwise it is discarded. The problems particular to a broadcast network occur in the allocation of the channel to a node for transmitting a packet. Different solutions are used for radio and satellite links. Each node is only able to communicate with each other node via the common channel, so some scheme is needed to coordinate transmission. The schemes that have been proposed and used are discussed here in increasing complexity and are compared for channel efficiency.

The simplest transmission technique is called pure aloha; when a node has a packet to transmit it does so immediately. Having transmitted the packet, the node waits for an acknowledgement. This is therefore a positive acknowledgement protocol. If an acknowledgement is not received within a time out period, the packet is assumed lost. Transmission collisions, which occur when two nodes transmit at the same time and thus interfere with each other's transmission, are detected by the time out mechanism. When a collision is detected, each node waits a period of time of random length before retransmitting the packet to try to avoid a further collision. Obviously, as the amount of traffic increases, the rate of collision will increase and more retransmissions will be needed. As the packets are retransmitted, more stations will have new packets to transmit causing more collisions, etc. Analysis has shown that a pure aloha scheme can only use a maximum of about 18% of the channel bandwidth. A node may transmit at any time, thus the maximum length of time the channel is wasted due to a collision is 2t, where t is the transmission time for one packet. The 2t period is the worst case, where one node begins transmitting just before the previous transmission is complete.

An improvement on pure aloha is slotted aloha in which the transmission channel time is divided into time slots of **t**. Each node is then only allowed to begin transmitting a packet at the start of a time slot. The nodes are kept in synchronisation by a time signal on the channel. Now if a collision occurs only one slot (of length **t**) is wasted, so the maximum efficiency rises to about 34% of the channel capacity. When a collision is detected, a transmitter must wait for a random number of time slots before retransmitting. When the traffic is light the wait can be quite short, but as the traffic load increases (indicated by the number of collisions) the waiting period should be increased.

From the aloha schemes it can be seen that it is collisions that cause problems, so a collision avoidance mechanism should improve efficiency. In packet radio networks a scheme known as carrier sense multiple access (CSMA) is used. When a node is transmitting all other nodes can receive the transmission, so they can avoid a collision by not transmitting themselves until the channel is free. A transmission is detected by the presence of the carrier signal in the medium. When a node has a packet to transmit it looks for the carrier; if there is no carrier the packet is transmitted. If the carrier is detected the node waits for a random length delay and tries again.

Even in a radio broadcast the signal from a transmitter takes a finite amount of time to reach all the receivers in the network. When two nodes find the channel free, they may both begin transmission because neither has heard the other one. This case is most likely to happen when two stations are waiting for the channel to become free. The length of time it takes to propagate the signal to all receivers is the time band in which collisions may occur, but it is less than the total packet transmission time. As with the aloha technique, the CSMA technique can be improved by dividing the channel time into slots and only allowing the transmission of packets to begin at the start of a time slot. The slot length is set to the propagation delay, not the packet transmission time.

The CSMA technique has been further refined by modifying the action of the node when the channel is busy. When the node samples the channel again and finds it free, it transmits its packet with a probability **p**, or waits for a further delay with a probability (1 - **p**). This is called persistent CSMA or p-persistent transmission. If **p** is high then the delay before transmission occurs is lower, but the possibility of collision increases if two stations are waiting after another station has finished. In persistent CSMA a trade off is made between channel efficiency and delay with the value of **p**. Channel efficiencies of about 80% may be achieved using these techniques.

Packet radio networks have a small delay between the start of a transmission and the detection of the transmission by all stations on the network. On a satellite broadcast network there is a very long delay between transmission and receiving, of the order of a quarter of a second. A satellite network operates by each transmitter sending its signal to the satellite (some 36 000 km above the surface of the Earth). The satellite then broadcasts the signal to all of the Earth stations, which may be spread over a very large area (figure 7.6). One satellite system currently used for packet switching connects nodes in England, Norway and North America using a satellite in stationary orbit over the North Atlantic. A different channel allocation technique is used on satellite broadcast networks because of the long propagation delay.

This satellite channel allocation technique involves making reservations for the future use of slots in the channel. The channel is divided into frames consisting of a number of reservation slots and a number of packet slots. There are many variations on the reservation technique, so only the principles are given here. A simplified diagram of a frame is shown in figure 7.7. Each reservation slot represents a packet slot in the second part of the frame. All ground stations are synchronised to the frame timing by the satellite transmission. During the first part of the frame the ground stations reserve slots for the packets they have ready by transmitting a marker during the reservation

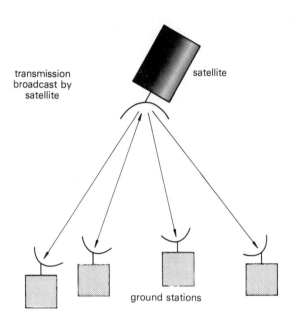

Figure 7.6 **Broadcast Satellite Network Topology**

slot time. When the reservation slot is heard back from
the satellite the ground station inspects the slot to
see if it contains its own marker. If so it can
transmit a packet in the corresponding packet slot in
the second part of the frame. This scheme uses some of
the channel capacity to avoid the collisions which
could reduce the network to a pure aloha scheme.

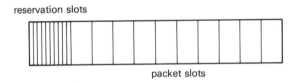

Figure 7.7 **Outline of a Satellite Network Frame**

Obviously more than one ground station may attempt to
reserve a particular packet slot by transmitting during
the reservation slot time. There are a number of
algorithms to overcome this, including allocating some
slots to busy stations. Thus if a station successfully
obtained a packet slot in the last frame, the same slot

is allocated to that station in the next frame without
competition. If an allocated slot is not used (the
station has no more packets to send) then the slot is
open for competition in the next frame. Usually there
are some slots that all stations can compete for in
every frame. Another mechanism involves using a central
allocation station to which each station sends its
requirements and the central station allocates the
slots. This has two disadvantages: firstly, the central
station becomes a weakness in the network reliability,
and secondly, the delay between requesting an allocation
and receiving the allocation may be of the order of 1 or
2 seconds before the packet can be transmitted.   A
chapter in the book by Kuo is dedicated to broadcast
satellite protocols.

7.3 Local Networks

A local, or private, network is a communication system
connecting computers in a small geographical area, say
less than a few kilometres between the furthest points.
The network is wholly owned and run by one
administration.

    There are currently two basic types of technology
used on such a network, these are
                cable, or bus, technology and
                ring technology.

    Whereas wide area networks and satellite networks use
nodes to separate the internal network switching from
the user hosts, local networks are meant to be as cheap
as possible and so the separate node computer is
omitted. In both local network technologies all the
computers are directly attached to the transmission
medium by a special interface, and all the interfaces
receive all the packets. The difference between a ring
and a bus system is the way in which the channel is
allocated. Local networks are designed for use in local
computing by allowing the interconnection of very small
computers, such as microprocessors, and peripheral
devices, such as line printers and disc storage units.
If the local network is to be useful, the cost of the
computer interfaces into the network channel has to be
low compared with the cost of the computer or

peripheral, and microprocessors are very cheap in computer terms. A widely forecast use of local networks is connecting word processors within a set of offices for the exchange of information and electronic mail. The cost constraints, the limited processing power of the small computers, and the protocols used on a local network are different from those used in wide area networks. A local network usually has a very high bandwidth channel of between 1 mHz and 10 mHz and a very low error rate, say one packet in several million might be corrupted. These characteristics enable the use of simple protocols. The lowest level protocol for using the transmission medium is built into the computer interface. The paper by Clark (in the November 1978 issue of the Proceedings of the IEEE) contains a good introduction to local networks.

Cable or Bus Networks

These networks usually use a length of co-axial cable, or an existing cable such as one used for closed circuit television (CCTV). The medium is used in a broadcast fashion, exactly as described in the previous section on broadcast networks. The channel allocation techniques vary slightly on the theme of the CSMA techniques, or on a centralised slot allocation. The most popular broadcast local network is the Ethernet system (see paper by Metcalfe and Boggs), developed by Xerox. The Ethernet principles can be used on any broadcast medium: radio, telephone lines, co-axial cable and optical fibres have all been used successfully. The Ethernet uses a base band signal, rather than a modulated signal, to simplify the broadcast transmitter and receiver. The Ethernet uses a modified CSMA channel access technique. To obtain the maximum efficiency from the broadcast medium an Ethernet transmitter can listen to its own broadcast to detect a collision (causing interference) and abort the transmission. This extra complexity is known as CSMA-CD (CD = collision detection) or listen-while-talk. As with the other CSMA techniques a station does not begin transmitting until the broadcast medium (or 'ether') is free. Two stations waiting for another station to finish a transmission will begin transmitting together, and thus interfere with each other. The collision is detected by the stations and they both

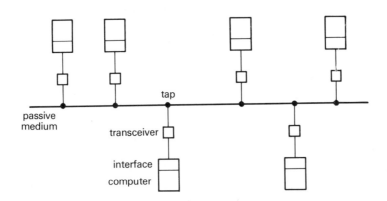

Figure 7.8 **Ethernet Broadcast Network Topology**

abort the transmission immediately. To enforce the
protocol a station that aborts a transfer then jams the
ether. After a collision each station waits for a
random time before trying again.

The CSMA-CD technique enables the Ethernet system to
obtain up to 95% of the broadcast channel bandwidth.
The improvement in performance over ordinary CSMA is due
to the stopping of transmission as soon as a collision
is detected. Note that no slots are used. Figure 7.8
shows an Ethernet configuration; the transceiver handles
all of the CSMA-CD access, including the retries and
delay calculation which is varied with the traffic load.
Thus only complete, and checked, packets are passed up
to the station interface and only one request is made
for a packet to be sent. Figure 7.9 shows the Ethernet
packet format: the shaded parts are handled by the
Ethernet hardware and not used by the station. The
checksum generation, and checking are carried out within
the hardware: bad packets are discarded. A time out
mechanism is used to retransmit packets that may have
been lost due to errors.

Ring Networks

The ring technique originated in the US. The idea was
then developed in parallel at Cambridge University in
the UK and at two research centres in the USA. The
version developed at Cambridge is known as the Cambridge

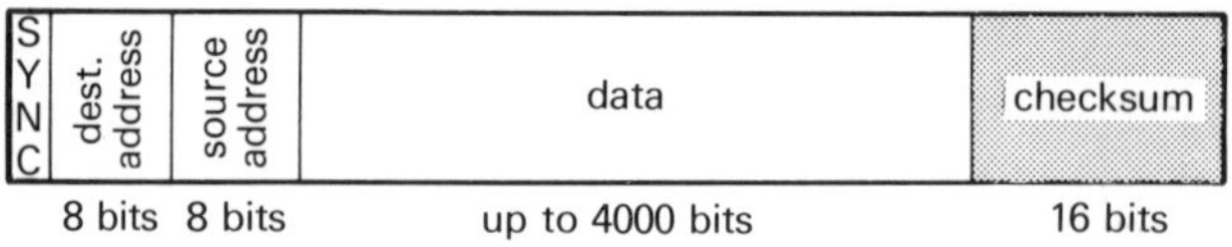

S Y N C	dest. address	source address	data	checksum
	8 bits	8 bits	up to 4000 bits	16 bits

Figure 7.9 **Ethernet Packet Format**

ring in the UK. The computer interface is divided into two parts: the repeater and the interface proper (sometimes called the station). A ring uses a twisted pair of wires as the transmission medium. However, to improve reliability, the repeater is powered from the ring and electrically isolated from the computer interface, so four wires are used to connect the repeaters. The four wires are used as two pairs for signalling and carry sufficient power for the repeaters. In this way the computer can be switched off and removed from the ring without switching off the repeater. Figure 7.10 shows the ring topology. With the ring the medium is terminated at each station, whereas in the cable network it is not. Each station is represented by a repeater, several of which are then connected together into a ring. The repeater is a simple device containing a shift register and some logic to detect certain conditions in the information being passed around the ring. The repeater normally passes any information received on to the next repeater, so transmission only occurs in one direction. When a station transmits data, the repeater transmits the information from the station instead of the information received from the previous repeater.

There are slight differences in the channel allocation mechanism used in the Cambridge ring and in those rings developed in the USA. In the Cambridge ring a fixed size mini-packet is used which constantly circulates in the ring, and a special station called a monitor is used to generate and maintain the mini-packet and provide the power for the repeaters. In the American versions a variable size packet is used which may be lost and regenerated as required by each repeater. The current format of the Cambridge mini-packet is shown in figure 7.11. Note that only 16 bits of information are carried in a ring mini-packet whereas

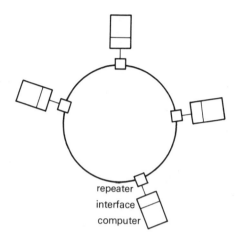

Figure 7.10 **Ring Network Topology**

the broadcast network packet may contain several hundred
bytes. The assembly of information into a block has to
be done by the computer. The monitor station also
provides a buffer if the ring is not physically long
enough to hold a complete mini-packet. The monitor
performs a check on the mini-packet each time it passes
to ensure that it is intact, and to replace it if not.
The monitor is an obvious weakness in the Cambridge ring
design so far as reliability is concerned; however,
experience so far has shown that monitor failures are
rare. The advantage of the monitor is that the
repeaters can be very simple (and therefore less likely
to fail) as well as cheap, which is the purpose of a
local network.

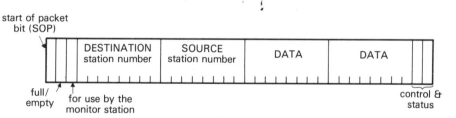

Figure 7.11 **Cambridge Ring Mini-packet Format**

To use the ring to send a packet of information, the station will wait until an empty mini-packet is detected by the repeater. When the full/empty bit in the mini-packet passes the repeater it is set to one. If the packet was already full no change has been made to the bit; if the packet was empty (full/empty bit = 0) the mini-packet is now reserved by this station. The repeater will use this mini-packet if the full/empty bit was received as 0. The addresses of the source and destination stations are placed in the address fields followed by the next 16 bits of the information that the station wishes to send; these are placed in the data field from the station buffer. The reserved mini-packet then travels round to all the other stations on the ring. Each station has a source select register in which an address is placed. If the source address in a mini-packet matches the contents of the source select register, and the destination address matches the station address, the data field is copied into the station receive buffer and the accept status is set at the end of the packet. If the packet is refused, or the destination station is busy, the destination repeater will set the appropriate value in the status bits at the end of the mini-packet. No other change is made by the receiving repeater, and all other repeaters will pass on the mini-packet unchanged. Special values which can be used in the source select register are 377 (octal) which means accept any source station address and 000 (octal) which means do not accept the data from any mini-packets.

When the mini-packet returns to the sending station the full/empty bit is reset to 0 and the status bits are checked to see if the information was accepted. As an error check, the station also reads back the 16 data bits and checks them against the data in its buffer. Having reset the full/empty bit, the station must now wait for another empty mini-packet before it can send the next 16 bits of information. In this way the now empty packet becomes available to successive stations around the ring and the packet slot is allocated in a round robin fashion.

The variable nature of packet traffic in a local
network makes it difficult to design a system that will
provide a very fast response, especially when there is
little traffic, and yet not become overloaded or unfair
when the traffic becomes heavy. The broadcast
techniques provide a low delay, especially in low volume
traffic, as the transmitter can usually send a packet as
soon as one is available. However as the volume of
traffic increases, the broadcast system suffers from
collisions and longer delays which can eventually lead
to an unstable situation. In the ring the channel is
allocated by means of a round robin mechanism so
collisions never occur, and during a burst of traffic
each station is able to continue transmitting with only
a larger delay. During periods of low traffic volume
the ring does introduce a delay while a station waits
for the empty packet to come round.

Proponents of both systems argue that because of the
very high bandwidth (1 to 10 million bits per second)
available on the channel, and the low processing power
of the computers attached to the local network, the
volume of traffic is nearly always low in a broadcast
network and the delay is negligible in a ring. Systems
have been proposed, based on the ring topology, that
attempt to provide the advantages of broadcast
techniques in low volume traffic periods but move to the
slot allocation mechanism of the ring during high volume
traffic periods. Most of the new systems attempt to
reduce the overhead of the Cambridge design which uses a
very small data field by having larger, usually variably
sized, packets but this invariably involves more complex
repeaters.

7.4 Summary

The various types of connection technology have been
divided, somewhat arbitrarily, into three areas: wide
area networks, radio and satellite broadcast networks,
and local area networks. The use of satellite and radio
media could be incorporated into a wide area network.
For instance, a project in the USA uses mobile vans with
terminals on a packet radio network to connect users to
a host via the ARPA network. The interconnection of
networks is briefly discussed in chapter 10. Satellite

links have been proposed to connect very distant parts of a wide area network to provide better end-to-end throughput because the channel bandwidth on a satellite is much greater than that available on land lines. The satellite delay is still a problem however.

Techniques for allocating the bandwidth of the transmission channel are the important differences between the three areas of network technology discussed above. The different techniques are required by the characteristics, such as delay and access, of the different physical media. Many organisations are installing local networks to distribute computing resources within a small area. Many of these local networks may also be connected to wide area networks via a common host.

8 The X25 Network Access Protocol

The protocols used in a computer network are the mechanisms by which the various entities: nodes, hosts, processes, and users, exchange information in a secure and controlled manner. Because of the number of entities involved, communications protocols are structured into layers, each layer having its own specific protocol. The purpose of a layer is to carry out communication for a higher layer using lower layers as carriers. Each layer allows communication between two similar entities, for example node to node, host to host, user to user. The boundaries between layers has been the subject of considerable debate in standards committees throughout the Western world. Various networks already implemented have defined their own protocols and therefore their own layers. New networks are trying to match the currently agreed layer architecture so that intercommunication will be possible through standard mechanisms.

Within any layer, a protocol has two common tasks: error control and flow control. Error control is concerned with detecting, and correcting, errors that may have occurred in the information being transferred. Flow control is concerned with managing the resources of bandwidth and storage so that no single user can monopolise these resources. This is usually achieved by keeping the sending and receiving rates of information transfer approximately in step.

This chapter contains a description of the X25 protocol. This protocol covers the 3 layers at the lower end of the layer hierarchy. X25 is an access protocol, which means that it is used between a host and a node (in most X25 networks the nodes are called exchanges) for the host to access the network so that communication between remote hosts is possible. The X25 protocol has been adopted by the CCITT as a standard,

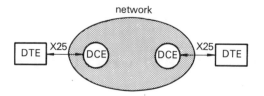

Figure 8.1 **DTE-DCE Arrangement**

which means that nearly all future networks will use it.
As well as describing the particulars of X25, the
principles of error and flow control will be shown and
the mechanisms used to implement them in each layer
explained. The description of level 2 is very detailed,
as this is the first consequential level to be met in
the bottom-up approach. The discussion of level 2
examines a number of problems which occur at many other
protocol layers. For instance, the mechanisms used at
level 3 for flow control and protocol synchronisation
are very similar to those of level 2, so less detail is
given in the level 3 explanation and references are made
to the level 2 mechanisms.

In the X25 parlance a host is called a DTE (Data
Terminating Equipment) and a node is called a DCE (Data
Communications Equipment). X25 provides a standard
mechanism for a DTE to access and use a DCE to transport
data across a network to a remote DTE via its remote
DCE. Figure 8.1 shows the DTE and DCE arrangement. The
protocol used between the DCEs within the network does
not have to be X25, but would probably be very close to
it. X25 is a virtual call rather than a datagram
protocol, although the intra-network protocol could be
either. The network implications for X25 implementation
are discussed in section 8.5. Datagrams and virtual
calls are compared in chapters 9 and 10.

8.1 Level 1 - The Physical Circuit

This level provides the physical communication by
specifying the electrical signals, voltages, plug shape
and pin assignment that the DTE needs to connect
physically to the DCE. In figure 8.2 the DTE/DCE
boundary is shown on the host side of the MODEM at the
host site. This would be the normal arrangement, as the

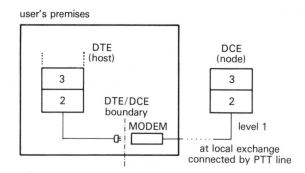

Figure 8.2 **DTE–DCE Boundary**

supplier of the network (usually the PTT) will provide
the MODEM link to the node (DCE) from the user's
premises. The actual specification of level 1 is
contained in the CCITT X21 recommendation. For
practical purposes the user will order a computer
interface to this standard which plugs straight into the
computer at one end and into the MODEM at the other.
The user will normally also be able to buy the software
necessary to handle the interface.

As the level 1 hardware is bought as a ready–made
unit, no further discussion of it is necessary. The
important information needed about level 1 is the type
of interface it presents to level 2, and the functions
it must perform. The level 1 will provide transport for
a bit stream from one site to another (remote) site.
The level 2 will present the level 1 with the bits which
are then delivered to a level 2 at the remote site. The
hardware of level 1 will also indicate if the physical
circuit is working correctly, that is whether the MODEMs
are switched on and able to exchange synchronised data.
So the interface has two parts

1. the sending and receiving of a serial bit stream

2. the control signals indicating the status of the
   physical circuit.

8.2 Level 2 – Link Level

The purpose of level 2 is to control the physical link between the two ends of the level 1 circuit to provide a reliable transfer of information for level 3 between the DTE and DCE. X25 level 2 uses a link control protocol based on the ISO HDLC (Higher Data Link Control) protocol. The advantages of using an existing protocol are greater than those to be gained from designing a new one. For instance, a new protocol would have to be adopted by a large number of people wishing to communicate; adoption of the protocol would then require a lot of effort. Other link protocols have been designed: **IBM** use one called **SDLC** (Synchronous Data Link Control) which is not dissimilar to HDLC and **DEC** have their own as well. The BSC protocol introduced in chapter 5 is also a link level protocol.

Information is passed from level 2 to level 1 in blocks called frames. The use of frames enables easier management of storage and error control. Each frame consists of some protocol information added by level 2, and possibly an information packet from level 3. The functions performed by level 2 are

1. Establish the link connection to a level 2 at a remote site (the DCE).

2. Transfer packets for level 3 securely, and in sequence.

3. Disconnect the link without loss of level 3 information.

To carry out these functions, the X25 level 2 uses three types of frame format. Figure 8.3 shows the details of the formats. The uses of each format is shown in the next section, but first the fields in the frames are detailed (the syntax of the protocol).

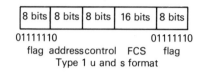

| 8 bits | 8 bits | 8 bits | 16 bits | 8 bits |

01111110   01111110
flag address control   FCS   flag
Type 1 u and s format

| 8 bits | 8 bits | 8 bits | n bits | 16 bits | 8 bits |

01111110   01111110
flag address control   data   FCS   flag
Type 2 I format

Figure 8.3   **Level 2 Frame Formats**

Flag Field

This is a unique 8 bit pattern (01111110) which marks
the beginning and end of each frame. The use of the
flag presents a problem: to ensure that the end of the
frame is correctly interpreted by the receiver, the flag
pattern must not appear anywhere within the data in the
frame. This means that the frame must be transparent to
the hardware looking for a flag to mark the beginning or
ending of a frame. The problem of transparency occurs
in all link level protocols as they all use special bit
patterns for synchronisation and for marking various
parts of the frame. In X25 level 2 the flag is used as
the level 1 synchronisation character (see chapter 2 on
synchronous character frames). To ensure that the flag
pattern does not occur within the frame, X25 uses a
technique called bit stuffing. The bit stuffing
technique involves the sender in inspecting the frame
contents prior to transfer to level 1. Whenever a
sequence of five 1s occurs a 0 is inserted. Thus
          ..0111111.. becomes ..01111101..
and
          ..0111110.. becomes ..01111100..
notice that the 0 is inserted regardless of the value of
the sixth bit. Bit stuffing in this way is easily
implemented by hardware and only increases the length of
the frame by 1 bit for every sequence of five 1s. As
the receiving hardware scans the incoming frame, a 0
following a sequence of five 1s is removed. If the
sequence of five 1s is followed by a further 1 then the
flag may have been found. The seventh bit is then
inspected: if it is a 0, the flag has been found
(01111110) whereas if the seventh bit is another 1

(01111111) then the frame is in error. Thus a sequence of seven 1s is used to abort the frame.

There are other ways of providing transparency, such as using escape characters, or bit counts, but none is quite so efficient and flexible as bit stuffing.

Address Field

This is really redundant in a point-to-point link. The intention in the HDLC protocol was to use this as an address for multipoint lines, but the present X25 recommendation does not include multipoint lines. However, X25 uses the field as an additional check in the protocol, as well as having the field ready should multipoint lines be considered in the future. The addresses used in this field allow commands and responses to be separated. The level 2 link can be thought of as two separate channels.

Channel A for transferring data from the network (DCE) to the host (DTE) and
Channel B for transferring data from the host (DTE) to the network (DCE).

Any frames relating to information flow from the DCE to the DTE carry the address A (11000000) including any frames from the DTE to the DCE relating to information transfer from the network to the host. Similarly for channel B (10000000). To help separate the channels, frames are divided into two classes: commands and responses. Commands always flow in the direction of information on a channel, responses flow in the opposite direction. Responses are obviously the receiver's replies to various commands.

Command Field

This 8 bit pattern determines the type of the frame, as well as being used for sequence numbering and acknowledgement. The command field has a different meaning for the three types of frame (information, supervisory, unnumbered). Figure 8.4a shows the command octet format for an **information frame**. A 0 in bit 1 indicates that this is an information frame. An

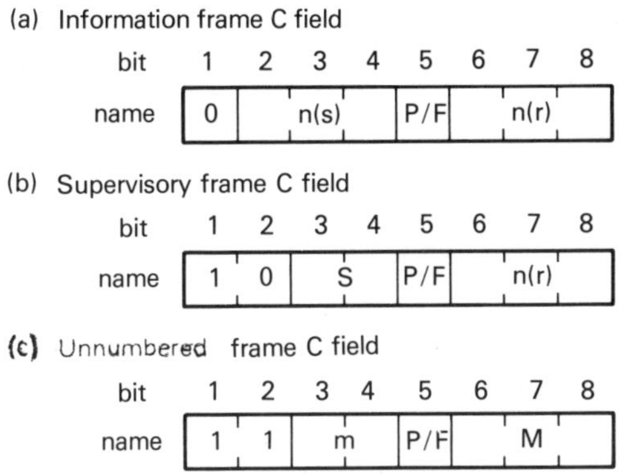

(a) Information frame C field

bit	1	2	3	4	5	6	7	8
name	0		n(s)		P/F		n(r)	

(b) Supervisory frame C field

bit	1	2	3	4	5	6	7	8
name	1	0	S		P/F		n(r)	

(c) Unnumbered frame C field

bit	1	2	3	4	5	6	7	8
name	1	1	m		P/F		M	

Figure 8.4   Command Octet Formats

information frame is the only type that carries a level 3 packet in the information field. Bits 2, 3 and 4 contain the sequence number of this frame, bits 6, 7 and 8 contain the acknowledgement number. The sequence number and acknowledgement number are used in the ARQ techniques explained in chapter 6 for error correction and flow control. Bit 5 is the poll/final (P/F) bit. This is set in a command frame as a poll bit and the receiver will set the final bit in any response frame that is a reply to a command frame with the poll bit set. The use of the poll/final bit enables the sender of a command to recognise the corresponding response frame.

Figure 8.4b shows the **supervisory frame** command field format. Bits 1 and 2 set to 10 indicate a supervisory frame. Bits 3 and 4 indicate which type of supervisory frame. Supervisory frames are not given sequence numbers as they do not contain any level 3 information, but they may be used to acknowledge information frames and so bits 6, 7 and 8 contain an acknowledgement number. Bit 5 is the poll/final bit which is the same as before.

Figure 8.4c shows the command field format for the **unnumbered frame**, so called because it contains neither sequence number nor acknowledgement number. Bits 1 and 2 set to 11 indicate an unnumbered frame and bit 5 is

Format	Commands	Responses	1	2	3	4	5	6	7	8
						Encoding				
Information transfer	Information		0		N(S)		P		N(R)	
Supervisory		RR-Receiver ready	1	0	0	0	F		N(R)	
		RNR-Receiver not ready	1	0	1	0	F		N(R)	
		REJ-reject	1	0	0	1	F		N(R)	
Unnumbered	SARM-set a synchronous resp.		1	1	1	1	P	000		
	DISC-disconnect		1	1	0	0	P	010		
		UA-unnumbered acknowledgement	1	1	0	0	F	110		
		CMDR-command reject	1	1	1	0	F	001		

Figure 8.5 **Command and Response Frame Summary**

the poll/final bit. The remainder of the bits are used to indicate the type of unnumbered frame.

Figure 8.5 summarises the various types of frames and indicates which are commands and which are responses.

Information Field

This field only occurs in I frames, it is the position in the frame where the whole level 3 packet is placed. The other level 2 fields provide an envelope for the level 3 packet during the level 2 transfer.

Frame Check Sequence

The FCS field is found by counting 16 bits back from the terminating flag. This is a 16 bit field to contain the CRC remainder used in error checking. The remainder is calculated using the CCITT recommended generating polynomial of $x^{16} + x^{12} + x^5 + 1$.

It is interesting to note that all the fields of the X25 level 2 header and the CRC are multiples of 8 bits. This makes transmission easier, because the 8 bit byte is the lowest common multiple of most modern computer word sizes, as well as being the character frame size for synchronous transfer. However the information field and the CRC may be increased by bit stuffing for level 1 transmission.

8.3 Operation of Level 2

This section describes the semantics of level 2, with the various commands and responses being explained in context. The level 2 at the DTE (host) end of the connection performs the protocol functions with the level 2 at the DCE, using the HDLC protocol on the level 1 physical connection.

Establishing the Link Connection

The first draft of the X25 recommendation contained a mechanism for establishing the channels A and B separately. This was called LAP (Link Access Protocol) and operated between the DTE (initiator) and the DCE. The LAP link establishment sequence was as follows. The DTE sends an SARM (Set Asynchronous Response Mode) unnumbered command to the DCE, with address B. When the DCE receives this it sets its internal variable $V(R)$ to 0, which represents the next expected sequence number. The DCE then responds with a UA (unnumbered acknowledgement). When the DTE receives the UA with address B it sets its $V(S)$ to zero, which is the next sequence number to be sent. Channel B is now initialised for data transfer. The DCE now sets up channel A using the same frame sequence but with address A. Figure 8.6 shows the sequence.

Unfortunately certain problems were found with LAP, so a second 'balanced mode' method was devised, known as LAPB. The LAPB method of initialisation sets up both channels simultaneously. The LAPB establishment is shown in figure 8.7.

In either method, once the link is established, data transfer may begin.

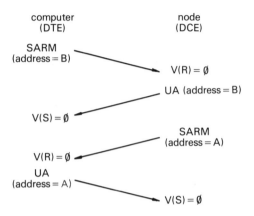

Figure 8.6 **LAP Link Setup**

Data Transfer

Level 2 should provide a sequenced, error-free transport of level 3 packets from the DTE to the DCE and vice versa. The method chosen is a Go-Back-N ARQ technique as described in chapter 6. As only 3 bits are allowed for the sequence number and acknowledgement number in the C field, the maximum window size is 7. In X25 the link level window size is fixed when the subscriber first applies to use the network. The operation of the data transfer allows the use of limited buffers at the sender (no more than 7) and no requirement for extra buffers to handle out-of-sequence frames at the receiver. The cost of the small buffer requirement is extra channel capacity taken up with retransmission. The use of X25 to connect hosts to networks would normally involve a fairly high speed circuit between the DTE and DCE. The limiting factor in performance is more likely to be the network and level 3, so a super-efficient level 2 is not necessary; thus simpler techniques, such as Go-Back-N, can be used.

The transfer of sequenced frames of information is straightforward but what makes the operation complex (and this applies to every protocol) is the handling of exceptions and errors. There are two basic errors that can occur during data transfer.

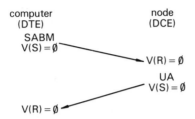

Figure 8.7 **LAPB Link Setup**

1. The frame check sequence indicates an error in the packet.

2. The packet appears to contain no transmission errors but the contents of the A and C fields are not correct.

In case 1 above the frame is thrown away and no further action is taken by the receiver. Obviously when a frame is discarded the next frame received is not the one expected. In case 2 there are a number of inconsistencies that can be classed as errors. The most common would be a sequence error where a previous packet had been lost, or discarded. To ensure that the frame sequence is maintained at the receiver, any frame that does not contain a sequence number matching that of the next expected frame variable, V(R), is an error. If the sequence number of the error frame is within the window, the receiver returns an REJ response to indicate, in the N(R) field, the frame from which the sender should retransmit. If the frame sequence number is not within the window then the sequence numbers of the two ends have become unsynchronised. The only way to recover from a synchronisation problem is to reset the sender and receiver to a known state. The CMDR (command reject) frame initiates a reset which is completed by going through the link establishment exchange. After a reset, the two end stations will be in a known, initial state. The reset procedure is used to recover from all errors other than the loss of an information frame. A reset may be caused by the receipt of a command or response that is not expected, for instance a UA if the data transfer is in progress, or the setting of the P/F

bit in a response when no command has been sent with
that bit set.

The flow control of the window ensures that the
sender cannot have more than a certain number of
outstanding frames, but if the receiver has taken all
the frames in a window, it must acknowledge them or the
sender will think the receiver has stopped. If the
receiver of a command does not reply within a certain
time the sender will retransmit the command, causing a
duplicate frame to exist. If, after a fixed number of
retransmissions, the receiver does not reply, the sender
will declare the receiver dead and give up the
connection. For this reason a receiver must return
acknowledgements for all frames as soon as possible, or
the link may be broken. A problem arises when the
receiver has filled up its buffers so that it cannot
take any more data, but has to reply to the sender.
There has to be a mechanism for the receiver to stop the
flow of data from the sender, without appearing to have
broken the connection by going quiet. In X25 level 2
there are two response frames for this purpose. The RNR
(receiver not ready) frame tells the data sender that
the receiver will ignore any further information frames.
Once the receiver has returned an RNR response to an
information frame, no more information frames are
accepted, but the $N(R)$ field in the header of any
further information frames is inspected so that
information frames in the opposite direction are
properly acknowledged. The RNR response only stops
information on one channel, the other channel is
unaffected. When the receiver has more buffer space, an
RR (receiver ready) frame is sent to inform the
information sender on that channel that more information
frames may be transmitted, starting at $N(R)$. Note that
both RNR and RR have acknowledgement numbers, $N(R)$. The
RR frame has another use: if the receiving station does
not have any information frames to be sent on the
opposite channel, the acknowledgements cannot be piggy-
backed, and the RR frame is then used to acknowledge the
information frames.

A receiver, especially a DCE (node), may not have enough buffers to take a full window for every level 2 link to which it is connected. Instead a statistical allocation could be used which assumes that not all links will be fully active at the same time and that the data is forwarded within a given time. When the network becomes busy this allocation means that a receiver may run out of buffers and need to use some technique to stop the flow of data from one or more links. Every frame, whether it is data or control, needs some buffer space for its receipt. If all the buffers are used up by one link then none of the other links will be able to continue transferring information. Also, if every buffer is allocated, there may be no more buffers to receive a control frame acknowledging a data frame and releasing buffer space! To avoid these problems, complex buffer allocation methods may be used. Normally, enough free buffers are always kept to receive at least one frame on each link so that control information can be exchanged even if data cannot. An information frame would be received, the control information used (for example N(R)), and then the frame discarded so that the buffer may be used again.

The loss of information frames due to buffer starvation means that information is lost not only because of errors in transmission, but also due to the internal operation of the nodes of a network, especially when the network becomes heavily loaded. These issues are taken up in chapter 10.

Link Disconnection

The mechanisms for closing the level 2 link are different for LAP and LAPB. Just as in link connection, LAP was the earlier version which allowed a possible deadlock situation to arise if the two channels were closed separately. In LAPB the channels are both closed in one exchange of DISC (disconnect request) and UA packets. Figures 8.8 and 8.9 show the different sequences for LAP and LAPB.

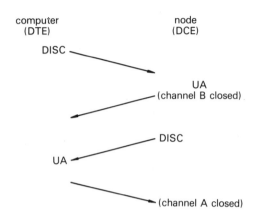

Figure 8.8 **LAP Link Disconnection**

8.4 Level 3 — The Network Level

The function of level 2 is to carry a level 3 packet
across a link. The function of level 3 is to carry a
piece of information from one host (DTE) to another via
intermediate network nodes. The transfer of the level 3
information will involve a number of level 2 links. The
X25 specification only covers the link between the DTE
and DCE, but we will assume a similar protocol is used
between each node of the network as well. Each level 3
packet contains a certain amount of level 3 protocol
information in a header, then possibly some user data
(from level 4). The major differences between level 2
and 3 are the use of addresses and logical channel
numbers. Most hosts will be connected to the network by
one level 2 link. This link then has to be used to
enable the host to communicate with several other hosts
by multiplexing logical channels on to the one physical
link. Level 3 is used to achieve this multiple
connection via a single link. Using level 3 a host
establishes a logical channel to another host by making
a connection request using the full address of the
remote host. When the connection is established it
becomes a logical channel with a unique number, the
logical channel number. Using the logical channel
concept, packets for several calls may pass across the
same level 2 link as they are all identified by a unique
channel number. At the DCE the channel number is used
to decide which route the packet will take. The logical

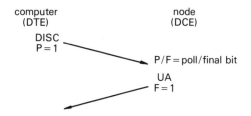

Figure 8.9 **LAPB Link Disconnection**

channel is in fact a virtual circuit.

Level 3 has the same basic functions to perform as level 2.

1. Connection establishment.

2. Data transfer.

3. Connection disconnection.

The difference for level 3 is that these functions are now carried out (apparently) between two hosts.

Packet Format

The level 3 headers are used to contain a variety of information, so they are not of uniform size like the level 2 frame headers. The level 3 headers are different for every type of packet, which makes the format quite complex. Figure 8.10 shows a general outline of a level 3 packet. The general format identifier (GFI) field indicates which format of level 3 header follows. The logical channel group number and logical channel number provide a 12 bit channel numbering field. Splitting the field may allow subdivisions to be used for, say, different services.

Call request and incoming call packets contain the address of the remote host (DTE). The addresses may contain fields indicating a particular process on a host as well as identifying a host. The address fields are of variable length, preceded by a byte count.

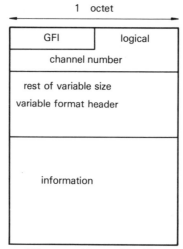

GFI = general format identifier

Figure 8.10 **General Outline of Level 3 Packet**

Connection Establishment

To begin a call, a host uses the full address of the remote host in a call request packet sent from the DTE to the DCE. The DCE will respond with either a call accepted packet if the request was successful, or a clear indication packet if the call was refused.

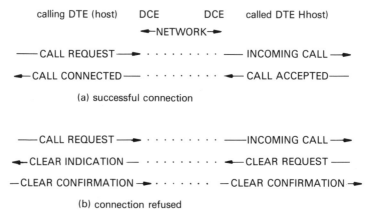

Figure 8.11 **Level 3 Call Opening (and Rejection)**

At the remote host the DCE will send an incoming call packet to the host to indicate that a remote call has been requested. The DTE receiving an incoming call packet will inspect the header to decide if the call is to be established or not. If the call is accepted a call accept packet is sent to the DCE; if the call is rejected a clear request is sent to the DCE. Figure 8.11 shows the two sequences. The channel number chosen for a new outgoing call by the DTE is the lowest available number. The channel number for an incoming call is chosen by the DCE as the highest available number. If the DTE and DCE agree on the channel numbers, and the DCE will accept the call, all subsequent packets on that call will only use that channel number, not the full address. A call has been established to a remote DTE when a host receives a call accepted packet having the same channel number as the call request packet. The call is established at the remote DTE when the call accepted packet is sent to the DCE.

X25 level 3 also has a datagram facility that allows a DTE to send a single packet to a remote DTE and receive a single packet in reply. This facility is provided by placing the information in the call request packet, and the reply information in the call reject packet. This is effectively the opening and closing of a call in a single packet exchange.

Information Transfer

Level 3 transfers data to the network in a sequenced stream using Go-Back-N ARQ. The techniques of sequence numbers, piggy-backed acknowledgements, RNR, RR and REJ responses are the same as for level 2, but they control the data flow across the network and into the remote host for each independent logical channel. The use of windows and sequence numbers was for error control in level 2 as the level 1 link was prone to errors. At level 3 the level 2 link is assumed to be error free so the emphasis is different. The windows and sequence numbers are now used primarily for end-to-end flow control. The receipt of acknowledgements allows more information into the network, while the window limits the number of data packets in flight at any one time.

Complete suspension of the data flow can be achieved by using a level 3 RNR, but the flow can be throttled back, or quenched, by the rate of acknowledgement.

Interrupt

An extra mechanism is used at level 3 to handle what is known as **out-of-band** transmission. Normal user data on an X25 virtual call is kept in strict sequence; this is called 'in band' transmission. However, a user application often requires a special signal which is not subject to the normal flow control. Such a signal is the abort character which a terminal user would type to stop a runaway program. X25 level 3 uses an interrupt packet to carry this out-of-band signal. The interrupt is not subject to the normal information flow control, the idea being that the interrupt could overtake information packets already in the network. The packet contains a field to indicate the cause of the interrupt, and it is up to the application to decide what to do both with the interrupt and any subsequent data. When the DTE sends an interrupt packet the DCE responds with an interrupt confirmation. The interrupt sequence is shown in figure 8.12. X25 permits only one interrupt to be outstanding on a logical call.

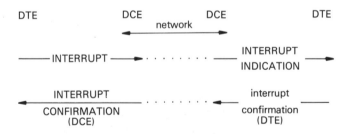

Figure 8.12 **Level 3 Interrupt Packet Exchange**

Resets and Restarts

In level 2 the reset was introduced as a mechanism for recovering from a protocol error where the two ends in the link became un-synchronised. The same thing can happen between the DTE and DCE at level 3, except that there are two areas where problems may occur.

The first problem is due to the information frames and sequence numbers becoming out of synchronisation on a single call. This may be detected by receiving a sequence number outside the window or an acknowledgement for a packet that was not sent. An error may also have been detected by a higher level protocol, perhaps due to a network failure. In these cases only the one logical channel is affected so a **reset** is used. This sets the level 3 sequence numbers to 0 at the DTE and DCE. The reset will also be propagated to the remote DTE–DCE pair. The reset can be initiated from either the DTE or DCE and requires the usual request–confirmation exchange. A reset may cause the loss of any information packets within the network so a higher level protocol will need to recover any lost data.

More drastic action is needed if the DTE and DCE become un-synchronised over global level 3 operation. An example is the choice of a channel number for a call request. If the DCE does not agree with the DTE over the chosen channel number (it should be the lowest free number) it means one of them thinks it has more logical calls opened than the other! The freeing of logical channel numbers correctly is the reason for the clear–request and clear–confirmation pair. When the whole level 3 needs resynchronisation a restart is initiated. This affects all the logical channels on the DTE–DCE link. A reset on the level 2 link is seen as a restart at level 3.

Call Disconnection

A DTE wishing to terminate a call issues a clear request packet, to which the DCE will respond with a clear confirmation packet when the call has been cleared in the DCE. This may involve waiting for the forwarding of any information packets still held there. When the clear confirmation is received the channel number is freed for further use. At the remote end the DCE will send a clear indication packet indicating that the remote host has closed, and no more information packets will follow. The remote DTE will respond with a clear confirmation packet when all outstanding information packets have been acknowledged.

Data Flow

The level 3 transport mechanism requires the data from the higher level protocols to be broken into packets for transfer across the DTE–DCE interface. The X25 recommendation specifies possible data lengths of 16, 32, 128, 256, 512 and 1024 bytes, where 128 is the preferred maximum. It is probable that the PTT networks will guarantee 128 byte data packets. This means a user message must be broken into 128 byte sequences, the last one being perhaps less than 128 bytes. To enable the receiver to reassemble a message from multiple packets, level 3 uses a **more data bit** (M) in the information packet header to indicate that the current packet is not the last one of a message.

Just as the level 2 and level 3 need to include control information in the frames and packets as well as information from the next higher level, it is likely that a higher level protocol would like to send control and data over level 3. The higher level protocol may decide to add the control bits to the front of messages it passes to level 3. However, level 3 provides a mechanism that allows a higher level protocol to multiplex data and control information on to the level 3 packet stream, thus maintaining the flow control and sequencing. This mechanism is the **Q bit**. Use of the Q bit is mentioned in the X29 terminal access protocol in chapter 9. The Q bit is set when the packet contains control information, and is clear when the packet contains data. Thus the higher level protocol can quickly separate control and data information when receiving level 3 packets.

8.5 X25 Implementation

An advantage claimed for X25 is that it only describes the host–to–node (DTE–to–DCE) interface. The network itself (internode) can use any convenient protocols, even completely different protocols, and the user would be unaware of them. In fact the proposed PTT networks are all planning to use X25, or variations, within the networks for node–to–node transfer. The arguments about virtual call and datagrams are taken up in the next chapter; the problem considered here is the implications

of two methods of implementing an X25 interface in a DCE
that produce quite different results for the user.   The
discussion will show that even standards have complex
problems of **meaning**.

The   two   methods   of   implementation   involve   the
mechanism for generating responses to various DTE
packets at level 3.   From the above description it can
be   seen   that   a   command   response   sequence   is   used
throughout level 3.   The X25 specification indicates
quite clearly what responses are required, but leaves it
up to the implementer to decide when, and under what
criteria, the responses are made.

Consider the implementation that produces the DCE
response as soon as the DTE's packet has been processed
at the (local) DCE.   This means the DCE's answer is sent
to the DTE at the same time as the original request is
forwarded across the network and well in advance of its
arrival at the remote DTE.   Such an implementation would
give a very quick response to the user host.   For
instance, on a call request, the call connect packet
would appear 'by return', and the DTE could immediately
begin sending data.   The DCE–DTE flow control would
ensure the DCE was not flooded with data, but large
amounts could be in transit within the network, before
the call has been established at the remote end.   This
implementation would give the host the appearance of
high throughput, as the DCE–DTE flow control would be
the   only   restraint.   If   the   remote   DTE   eventually
refused a call the local DCE would merely have to clear
the call.   The transfer of data is a bit more difficult;
for   instance   if   the   DTE   receives   a   level   3
acknowledgement for a data packet, does this mean that
the remote DTE has received it, or only that the local
DCE has?   To be consistent in this implementation it
would have to be the latter, so the DCE has taken on the
responsibility for delivery of that data.   A higher
level protocol would be needed, with its own flow
control, to handle the host–to–host transfer.

This implementation has the effect, mentioned above, of apparently providing a fast throughput. A host may be able to open a call (to the local DCE), send data, and close the call, before the remote DTE has received a packet. The host will also see a fairly rapid data rate once a call has been made. The network, however, will contain a large amount of unacknowledged packets as the DTE-DCE flow control will accept packets as fast as the DCE can forward them into the network. This makes end-to-end flow control in the network difficult and can quickly lead to congestion.

In the second implementation we only allow the DCE to respond to the DTE when the response from the remote DTE has been received by the local DCE. This is the format assumed in the diagrams showing packet exchanges in level 3. Thus a call request from a host is forwarded by the DCE which then waits for the call accept from the remote DTE before replying to the local host with a call accepted packet. This gives the host an impression of a long delay. In fact the delay is the round trip to the remote host, plus processing. The data transfer is also affected by the DCE not acknowledging any level 3 packets until the acknowledgement from the remote DTE has been received. This end-to-end use of the level 3 protocol reduces the amount of processing required from higher level protocols. The sending DTE will only be able to have a window of packets outstanding which will represent the maximum number of data buffers which the whole network will need for the call. This makes the resource management within the network easier and is less likely to produce congestion. The cost is the lower performance seen by the user. Each packet takes longer to be acknowledged, thus reducing the throughput. There is also the problem of gaps; when a window full of packets is sent rapidly, followed by a delay until the first acknowledgement comes back. This 'bursty' mode of operation gives the network an uneven response and is difficult for both the host and DCE to manage. Throughput, delay and congestion are discussed further in chapter 10.

The current X25 recommendation allows a subscriber (DTE) to set a D bit in a data packet at level 3. This bit requires the acknowledgement to have end-to-end significance, as in the previous example above. The D bit is an option, which means a network does not have to implement it.

8.6 Summary of X25

Although X25 appears to provide a standard for interfacing a host to a network, it suffers in that it only defines the interaction between the host and its local network node. The host-to-host transfer seen through X25 can be very different depending on how the protocol is implemented. There appear to be redundant features in flow control, connection and disconnection, as both level 2 and level 3 are only defined across the DTE-DCE interface. However a network using X25 throughout can make more use of the level 3 flow control on logical calls.

9   End-to-end Network Protocols

Chapter 7 introduced some of the technology used in computer networks and chapter 8 covered a 'low level' access protocol, X25. This chapter in concerned with the higher level protocols, which are implemented in hosts for host-to-host communication.

9.1 Protocol Heirarchy

The relationship between the protocol levels discussed in chapter 8 and those discussed here can be seen by examining the protocol level architecture proposed by the International Standards Organisation (ISO). This is intended to be a framework into which new protocol standards can be placed.

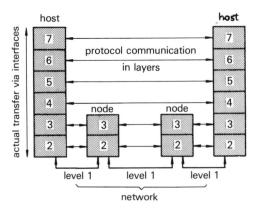

Figure 9.1   **Protocol Layers**

The ISO reference model is biased towards protocols based on X25, and because of this, protocol hierarchies based on other mechanisms (such as those used on the ARPA network) do not fit the proposed model very well. This does not mean that one way is correct, merely that there is more than one way of designing a protocol hierarchy. The ISO model has 7 levels,

```
level     1 physical circuit level
          2 link level
          3 network level
          4 transport level
          5 session level
          6 presentation level
          7 application level
```

The first 3 levels map exactly into X25. The other 4
levels are discussed below, and figure 9.1 shows the
levels diagrammatically.

Transport Level

This level separates the host from the network, level 3,
by providing interprocess communication rather than
host-to-host connection. A transport level connection
may exist over several networks, each of which will have
its own level 3 and may be different in some respects.
The transport level is responsible for the safe transfer
of a message, or data stream, from one application
process to another; as processes run on hosts this level
is only implemented on the hosts. Level 4 provides
addressing to a user application (rather than a host as
in level 3), sequencing (so that the data arrives in the
same order it was sent), multiplexing of connections and
some error and flow control.

Session Level

This level is responsible for the management of
resources used by the network applications, such as the
operating system, the use of buffers, and the
interprocess communication interface between the
applications process and the transport level process.
Address mapping between network addresses and the actual
processes is the concern of this level.

Presentation Level

The application or user process will not want the full
generality of a network but a specific service such as a
file transfer, or on-line access via a terminal, etc.
This level is concerned with mapping the user's
requirements into network actions. As this is the area
of mapping the user's view of the network into the

actual facilities, it is the level at which such features as device independence, address to service mapping, and virtual terminals are implemented. Many special protocols are implemented at this level for specific functions such as file transfer, message service, interactive use, etc.

Application Level

This level contains the processes within the host computer that are capable of using a network, or the human user at a terminal. It may be a language with network facilities, or a standard set of commands for terminal usage over the network. As all work in a computer is achieved by an active process, it is convenient to think of the process as the beginning and end of the network connection, especially for addressing purposes. However, all processes must work for someone, so it is reasonable to think of a human user beyond the application process.

9.2 Datagrams and Virtual Calls

One of the interesting debates among network designers is about the distribution of responsibility between the network (at level 3) and the host (at level 4) for certain facilities, such as flow control and sequencing of data. Thus there are two quite different schemes for transporting packets across the network at level 3, one involving datagrams and the other virtual calls.

The datagram scheme treats each packet as a separate unit. Once in the network it is forwarded to its destination by the best possible route available at the time. If a message is broken into multiple packets, the different packets may travel through the network by different routes and consequently arrive in a different order from that in which they were transmitted. The receiver will have to assemble the packets in their original order and detect any that are missing. If the original message only consists of one packet, and the packet is lost, or duplicated, then the transport level (level 4) must detect this and recover it. Each datagram, as the single packet is called, carries the

full source and destination address.   The advantages of
datagrams are threefold

1. The routing in the network can be very flexible, so
   that dynamic routing can be used with datagrams,
   which gives much better overall network reliability.

2. The network implementation is simpler than that
   needed for virtual calls.   This involves cheaper
   software for the nodes.

3. The transport level will have some error and flow
   control anyway, so datagrams do not duplicate this.

   A virtual call, on the other hand, is a mechanism for
establishing a 'connection' through a network between
two entities so that they can exchange data.   Once a
virtual call is established, resources are allocated so
that the entities know the information transfer may take
place.   The data packets are routed from node to node by
a route decided at the time the call was established.
Once the call is established the packets use a call
identifier instead of the full addresses as the route is
fixed.   The call mechanism ensures that the data is
delivered in the correct sequence and, as long as the
call is maintained, no data is lost.   The advantages of
a virtual call are

1. the data is delivered across the network in
   sequence, reducing the reassembly buffer space

2. end-to-end flow control on a call is implemented
   within the network

3. data packets on the call do not need to carry full
   addresses.

   The argument of datagram versus virtual call is one
of deciding what functions should be implemented in
level 3 and what are the desired characteristics of a
network.   The functions concerned are sequencing and
flow control, addressing and routing.   Virtual calls

restrict the type of routing that can be implemented, but provide a better interface for the network user because more functions are implemented in the lower levels. On the other hand, datagrams are more flexible and easier to implement on the nodes. The decision is not easy, and in practice is more complex than this discussion suggests.

9.3 Transmission Control Protocol

The virtual call access protocol, X25, was described in detail in chapter 8. Although X25 is very important as a standard, it is not the only way of implementing network protocols, and different techniques will be needed for networks with different requirements from those provided by the PTTs. This section briefly describes the Transmission Control Protocol (TCP) and the type of low level network it uses. The paper by Cerf and Khan provides a good dicussion of the reasoning behind TCP. TCP is a host-to-host protocol that roughly corresponds to the transport level in the ISO hierarchy model.

The TCP was designed for use on networks providing the minimum facilities to a host. Such a network would be datagram based in which packets are sent and received independently. The network would perform no sequencing or end-to-end flow control and packets may be lost or duplicated without notification. The TCP implementation would need to recover lost data, re-sequence data, detect duplicate data, and apply end-to-end flow control, all within a reasonable overhead. TCP has been quite successfully implemented on some very small computers.

TCP is mainly implemented on computers connected to the ARPA network. The ARPA network itself provides fully sequenced and controlled data flow for its hosts. However, other networks attached to the ARPA network do not provide such facilities, so traffic passing between these networks needs a protocol such as TCP. It is worth adding that TCP was designed for use in a multinetwork environment where no assumptions could be made about any single network.

Flow Control and Acknowledgement

The flow control and acknowledgement are implemented with sequence numbers and windows, although the scope of these is different from X25. Each 8 bit byte is given a sequence number so that successive bytes have successive sequence numbers. The sequence number in the TCP packet header is the sequence number of the first data byte in the packet. This enables the acknowledgement of variable amounts of data and allows for variable sized packets. Data is only accepted if it falls in the range of expected sequence numbers, which is from the last acknowledged byte (left window edge) to the left window edge plus the window size. Data is acknowledged by returning the sequence number of the last byte accepted by the receiver, and this includes all previous bytes. The sequence numbering is also used to acknowledge various TCP protocol commands. The commands themselves are represented by single bits in a command byte in the TCP header. If the bit is set, the command is included in the packet and is given a sequence number. Commands are seen as occurring before data in the packet, so the sequence number of a packet covers not only the data but also any commands in the header. Each separate command bit set is given a sequence number. The commands are always processed in a defined order so a number of bits may be set in a single packet. If a reply is sent to acknowledge any data bytes in a packet it automatically acknowledges any command bits from the packet. The format of the TCP header is shown in figure 9.2.

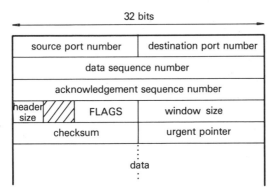

Figure 9.2 **TCP Packet Header Format**

The end-to-end flow control is achieved by adjusting the size of the window. Each TCP packet contains an updated window size from the receiver; if the window is zero, the sender may not send any more data until a non-zero window is received. By varying the size of the window a receiver can completely control the flow of data on a TCP connection to suit its own rate. The result of this design is that only one TCP packet format is needed.

Out-of-band Data

The need for out-of-band data was shown in the X25 protocol. TCP provides quite a different mechanism which was introduced because of the needs of a local network. The mechanism uses an **urgent pointer,** for which there is a field in the TCP header. If the urgent bit is set in the command byte, the urgent pointer field contains the sequence number of a byte which is to 'start an interesting sequence'. Normally a user would skip over all data up to that byte. An urgent pointer can point past the end of the packet in which it is included. The use of **urgent** is application dependent.

9.4 Comparison of X25 and TCP Protocols

The obvious comparison is that X25 is a virtual call protocol, while TCP is datagram based. The TCP protocol provides a more sophisticated end-to-end protocol than X25 level 3; a transport level protocol above X25 level 3 has been proposed which uses the same mechanisms as level 3. An observant reader will point out that TCP is an **end-to-end** protocol whereas X25 is only an **interface** protocol, but in terms of the protocol mechanisms, X25 could be used for end-to-end control as shown in the section on X25 implementation (section 8.5). A piece by piece comparison of protocols is not really possible as the architectures are different, but some comparison of techniques to achieve the same effects is reasonable.

Network Flow Control

Let us assume an X25 network that uses an X25 protocol for node-to-node traffic. X25 forces each node to maintain the sequence of transmission right across the network, whereas the TCP packets may take different routes as well as overtake each other due to retransmissions etc. The orderly flow of X25 data packets does mean that the network resource management will be easier, but not so flexible as that possible in the TCP network.

End-to-end Operation

The X25 protocol delivers the data packets in sequence to the host by using network bandwidth and node processing to ensure sequenced transmission; this is the concept of a virtual call. The TCP network uses free flowing datagrams to get a better throughput, but the host has to sequence the data, detect multiple copies and implement the entire TCP protocol without help from the nodes. This was one of the advantages (having the nodes do some work for hosts) that led the PTTs to choose a virtual call protocol for X25 so that customers could connect to the network with less software effort. However, the X25 host will still need some high level protocols and yet will not see the higher performance from datagrams.

An interesting technique to compare is the X25 interrupt using a separate packet format and exchange handshake against the TCP urgent mechanism to implement out-of-band signalling. Earlier versions of TCP did use a mechanism nearer to the X25 interrupt, so the urgent pointer might be considered a later development.

The differences between these two network protocols reflect on the users only marginally. Each protocol architecture was designed from different constraints but this underlines the fact that there is no 'correct' protocol as yet, and if there are two ways of doing something there must be others. The problems of making two protocols compatible is discussed in the next chapter, when the interfacing of networks is considered.

9.5 Network Applications Protocols

Both TCP and the X25 interface protocol are host-to-host protocols designed to carry data for higher level protocols that support various applications. Different applications will have different requirements from the

network, so they will need different high level
protocols. Two applications and their protocols are
discussed below: file transfer and terminal access.
These two applications have completely different
requirements, although the interface to the lower level
is exactly the same. When discussing higher level
protocols it is assumed that some transport level exists
above X25 level 3 that provides the facilities of TCP,
even though level 3 does provide many functions of a
transport level already. A chapter in the book by Kuo
is dedicated to file transfer, terminal and RJE
protocols.

File Transfer

The file transfer application uses a remote file store
or file handling system and the transfer of a large
volume of data involving a number of packets. The first
problem is the remote file store. As with an operating
system, a file transfer protocol (FTP) needs to be
device independent, but it also needs to be computer
independent in that different computer systems have
different file store conventions, particularly in naming
files. The system independence is achieved by having a
conceptual file store which is mapped into the actual
file system by the FTP protocol implementation; this is
the presentation protocol. An FTP has two phases in its
operation. The first is an interrogation which maps the
user's request to the conceptual file store into a
request to the physical file store, and which takes the
form of a dialogue between the originating FTP process
and the FTP process at the physical file store. If the
dialogue is successful, the second phase is entered,
which is the transfer of data. As a reliable transport
level is used, the FTP does not need too much flow
control or error control; indeed, these may be optional.
However, the FTP may include some mechanisms to recover
from a network problem (such as a reset) without
repeating the entire access sequence. An FTP protocol
is not symmetrical; there is one process requiring
access to a file store that will always initiate the
action, and another process at the file store (sometimes
called a server) which will handle and attempt to serve
requests. An attempt has been made to establish a
network independent file transfer protocol as a

standard, certainly for X25 based networks. The FTP
data transfer will be a large number of maximum sized
packets for which, although requiring a good service,
the delay and throughput are not critical. Where a
choice of service is available for a file transfer, a
high throughput is more important than a low delay.

Terminal Access

Terminal access protocols are used to enable a user at
an asynchronous terminal to access a remote host across
a network as if the user were connected directly to the
host. As well as the considerable differences between
packet   communication   and   asynchronous   terminal
communication there are the differences between the
various terminals themselves that can be used to access
a host. The major problem to be overcome is the fact
that most terminals cannot handle a full packet
protocol. Some intermediary processor must therefore be
used   to   handle   asynchronous   character-at-a-time
terminals on one side, and synchronous packet networks
on the other. Such a processor is called a packet
assembler and disassembler (PAD) on X25 networks and a
terminal interface processor (TIP) on the ARPA network.

The differences between various physical character
terminals and the different ways computer systems handle
the terminals could be a major hurdle to a standard
terminal access method. The problem is solved by using
a virtual terminal technique, similar to the virtual
file store used by an FTP. A virtual terminal has a
minimum set of characteristics – such as line length,
form feed operation, special character operation – and a
default value for each characteristic (parameter): for
instance 80 characters per line, no form feed operation,
etc. Using this virtual terminal each PAD, user and
host computer has a common basis from which they can
adapt the basic 'virtual terminal' into one that suits
their type of operation.

There are at least two ways of implementing a
terminal access protocol based on the virtual terminal.
On the ARPA network a protocol called TELNET uses an
extensible approach. On initial connection neither the
TIP nor the host computer makes any assumptions about

the terminal operation, other than the use of a standard character set. After connection, a negotiation is carried out regarding any specific characteristics, such as which will perform the echoing. The negotiation protocol allows the TIP, or the host, to ask for features, or to offer features, and for the other end to accept or refuse them. The protocol used for the negotiation allows a terminal or host to support very extensive features, including graphics, but only those available both on the host and the terminal will be agreed on. The negotiation is symmetrical between the host and the TIP.

A second method has been proposed for use on X25 based networks, such as PSS. The virtual terminal is described by a set of parameters which may take on specified values. The parameters and their values are described by a protocol called X3. There are at present twelve parameters defined, although this number will probably increase. Use of this parametric approach limits the features supported to those defined, and requires each PAD, host and terminal to support them. The PAD keeps a table showing the present values of each parameter for every terminal connected to it. A second protocol, X28, defines the commands used by a terminal operator to open a call, disconnect a call and vary some parameter values. A third protocol, X29, defines the control packet format used between the PAD and the remote host regarding the parameter values, and changes in the values. X29 uses the Q bit of the X25 level 3 data packet to differentiate control information and ordinary data. The ordinary data is the characters to be passed between the terminal and the application process on the network host.

The lack of negotiation in the X3/X28/X29 mechanism reduces the complexity of the protocol, which makes implementation cheaper. The TELNET protocol is more flexible and new features can be added more easily. This is another example where a trade off is available between cost and flexibility.

The terminal protocol is naturally divided into two parts, the presentation level which includes the commands and responses used by the user at the terminal to operate the protocol, and the session level used between the local processor (PAD, TIP) and the remote host to convey the commands and responses, as well as the characters normally transferred between an on-line user and the host.

On the TELNET protocol used on the ARPA network a single stream of 8 bit bytes is used. When a command or response is to be transferred, an escape character is used (377 in octal) to indicate that the next byte is a command or response and not a data character.

On an X25 network, X29 is the session level protocol. All data characters are placed in packets with the X25 level 3 Q bit clear. All control packets (containing parameter setting and changes) are placed in packets with the Q bit set. Thus it is easy to distinguish data and control packets. Because X29 uses X25 directly (no transport layer) it is limited to use on X25 networks. Protocols based on the principles of X29 are being proposed that use some transport service between the network and character protocols.

There are problems with a terminal access protocol, such as echoing of the typed characters, responses from the host, and the operating system control language for various computer systems. A terminal access protocol is not very efficient on a packet switched network as normally only a few characters are sent in each data packet, producing a large protocol overhead from lower levels. However on the ARPA network a large proportion of the traffic is due to the popularity and ease with which terminal users can access remote hosts. The terminal access traffic is characterised by small amounts of data in each packet requiring a fast response (low delay) from the network in order to maintain a suitable dialogue for the human user between the terminal and the remote computer.

9.6 Summary

The higher level protocols in a network protocol hierarchy support end-to-end communication over the network, or networks. The TCP protocol enables an interesting comparison to be made between two network protocol approaches which indicates that protocols will continue to evolve in the future.

The outline of two high level protocols serves to emphasise the different requirements of various network applications. The file transfer protocol uses bulk transfer with the emphasis on throughput rather than delay, whereas the terminal access protocol is characterised by small amounts of data (a few characters) requiring low delay. Some of the problems and considerations of the two protocols extend the area of discussion on alternatives in protocol design. The use of a **virtual file store** for FTP and a **virtual terminal** for terminal access represents a common solution to the problem of the incompatibility of devices and computer systems that are found on computer networks.

10   *The Network as a System*

This chapter is concerned with a packet switched network as a system. To provide efficient management of the communications hardware a packet switched network can be viewed as a resource management system. The user requirements of access and throughput are obtained by management of network resources such as buffer space and bandwidth. The expanding topic of network interconnection is briefly introduced.

10.1 Resource Sharing

One of the original intentions of general computer communication networks was to allow resource sharing between computers (hosts). For instance, one computer may have a special output device, such as a microfilm plotter device for producing slides, another may have a fast array processor and so on. A user wishing to perform complex computations and then output the results on to a slide, would either have to find a computer having both facilities or physically transfer the output data between computers via some common medium (if any exists!). A network allows the two computers to be connected so that the sharing of resources among users provides a better service. This sharing by using the network costs less than providing each project with its own resources. This is not only much cheaper, but it also means that projects have access to resources that they could not justify on their own. A public packet switched network, such as PSS, will be concerned with information transfer, but the resource sharing it will allow will be a major justification for the expense of interfacing to, and using, such a network.

An operating system on a timeshared computer is a resource management system. It manipulates system resources such as memory, CPU time, and peripheral access, to provide a user with a service. The user sees the service in terms of how easy it is to obtain access to the resources, and how well the system responds to commands. The software and protocol organisation of a computer network perform the same function, for both hosts and user processes wishing to use the network.

A packet switched network has two major resources that require management. These are the buffer space within the nodes and the bandwidth of the communication lines connecting the nodes. In chapter 7 it was shown that by transferring information in small packets the allocation of buffer space and bandwidth can be handled more easily than in message switching. The packet switched communication line is multiplexed between the packets, which provides more efficient use of the communications bandwidth than in circuit switching. The nodes in a packet switched network act as concentrators. A similar multiplexing mechanism was discussed in chapter 4 where character multiplexing was introduced. Packet switching is in effect statistical time division multiplexing of packets, rather than characters. The statistical aspect is very important, just as in the character system; the network will expect variations in traffic level, but over a long period of time the load will average out to a level which the network can handle. To manage the fluctuations each node has storage in which packets can be queued up waiting for their turn on the transmission line. When there is little traffic the queues will be short, but as the traffic increases the queues will become larger. If there is too much traffic at a node the node runs out of storage and packets have to be discarded, unless some flow control is exercised within the network.

An analogy can be made with a doctor's surgery where the doctor can see the patients at a specified rate (fixed bandwidth). After the surgery opens the queue in the waiting room grows. If the queue grows so large that the room is full, new people arriving will probably not bother to stay. Eventually the rate of people arriving falls off and the doctor begins to catch up – the queue goes down. This corresponds to a network node receiving a rush of packet traffic where packets can only be forwarded on a transmission line at a set rate. The use of storage to buffer a surge in traffic is the

hallmark of a concentrator. An important problem for a
network is to avoid filling all the buffers. A possible
solution is not to accept any packets from hosts until
there is room for them in the network: this point is
taken up in section 10.3.

This model of a network, as the interconnection of
store and forward concentrators by fixed bandwidth
channels, enables the derivation of some basic
characteristics of a packet switched network.

1. **Delay**
There will be a small delay to each packet due to
the time taken for the information to be transferred
along the transmission channels. The major part of
the delay seen by network users will be that caused
by queueing of packets in the nodes. The delay is
the time difference between a packet entering the
network and the packet leaving the network at the
destination. Most of the delay in a network is
caused by the store and forward operation of the
nodes. As each packet has to be completely received
into the node storage before being processed, even
in a lightly loaded network there will be delays.
The actual delay experienced by any packet will
depend on the size of the packet itself as this
reflects its transmission time, and the size of the
queues which in turn depends on the traffic level at
the node. The delay characteristic for a network
will therefore fluctuate depending on local as well
as overall traffic levels. Obviously the number of
node–to–node hops made by a packet traversing the
network will affect the delay seen by a user.

2. **Throughput**
This is the rate at which the sender can transmit
packets into the network on a particular connection.
The maximum throughput will depend on the bandwidth
of the communication lines and the processing speed
of the node computers. The actual throughput is
enmeshed with the network and host–to–host flow
control mechanisms which ensure that the host and
network are not overloaded by packets they cannot
handle. As most flow control mechanisms use

acknowledgements, which are themselves subject to delay, the throughput on a particular connection will also be a function of the network traffic levels. The throughput will fluctuate from the (finite) maximum, possibly down as far as zero for a network failure.

3. **Packet Failures**
   Due to the impossibility of having completely secure transmission, packets may be lost, or duplicated as a result of attempts to prevent loss by using time outs.

4. **Finite Storage**
   The network nodes have only a fixed number of buffers available. Any node that fills all of its buffers cannot accept any more traffic until some of the packets have been forwarded and accepted by the next node. Two full nodes trying to send to each other cannot do so − a situation known as deadlock.

The characteristics that most affect the user of a network are the delay and throughput. The node software has to allocate the node buffers and channel bandwidth throughout the network to provide a low-delay high-throughput transmission system with as little error as possible. Within the network the techniques used in flow control and routing enable the network to respond as a system to provide the best service to the user.

10.2 Throughput and Delay

The service characteristics of throughput and delay are linked by the traffic load. When the traffic is very light the delay will be minimal and the throughput maximal. This assumes that the receiving host can take the packets as fast as the network presents them and the acknowledgements from the receiving host do not arrive at the source host after the last packet in the window has been transmitted. The storage problems in a network occur when the receiver cannot take packets as fast as the network can deliver them. Packets build up in queues, firstly in the receiving node, and then back into the network nodes, until all the queues have been

filled up in the sending node.   If all the queues were
allowed to be filled up by one connection, the network
would not be sharing resources in a satisfactory way.
As the queues (containing packets from several calls)
fill up, the nodes do not have enough empty buffers to
accept incoming data packets.

The situation is similar to a busy city centre:
during the night there is very little traffic so cars
crossing the city experience very small delays.   During
the rush hour, the traffic load increases and the cars
begin queueing up at traffic lights and junctions with
the consequent delays.   The delays grow larger as the
traffic and queues grow.   In a packet network, as the
delays grow the data packets take longer to reach their
destination.   Furthermore the acknowledgements take
longer   to   return,   which   reduces   the   connection
throughput because of the window mechanism used in the
host-to-host protocol.

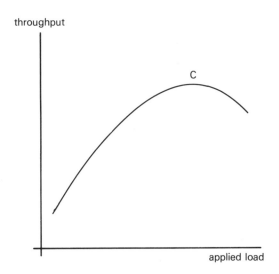

Figure 10.1   **Network Throughput Versus Network Load**

The   theoretical   relationship   between   the   total
network throughput and the total network traffic load is
shown in figure 10.1.   The effective throughput rate
increases as more traffic is applied, up to a certain
point at which the network becomes congested because the

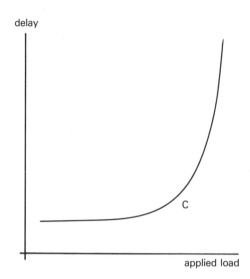

Figure 10.2   **Network Delay Versus Network Load**

total input of packets exceeds the packet delivery rate. When the network becomes congested, the packets are forced to wait in buffers and the throughput falls below the optimum.

The theoretical network delay and traffic load relationship is shown in figure 10.2. The delay increases slowly at first as the traffic increases because the queue sizes are not affected except in localised cases. When the congestion point is reached, the delay increases rapidly as the queues fill up. The point marked **C** in figures 10.1 and 10.2 represents the point at which congestion begins to affect the network performance.

10.3 Congestion Avoidance

The network as a system will attempt to avoid congestion by using routing and flow control to allocate the finite network resources. Flow control is effected at each protocol level: between nodes, between nodes and hosts, and between hosts (although X25 asserts host-to-host control via level 3 of the host-to-node access protocol). The purpose of network flow control is to avoid allowing any one host to dominate the allocation

of resources. The flow control procedures used in most
protocols are also used to control transmission errors
and recover from them, as discussed in chapter 6. The
use of acknowledgements and windows allows the various
levels to control the rate of acceptance of packets and
to try to match this with the rate at which packets are
leaving the network. As with any feedback control
system, the source and receive rates will not be in
absolute synchronisation, but over a period of time the
two rates should balance out. Flow control techniques
have already been covered generally in chapter 6, and
those for X25 in chapter 8.

Routing is a mechanism the network uses to manage
resources globally in the network. Under-used nodes and
lines can be detected and used to spread the load from
heavily used areas of the network. Once a routing table
has been built, each node will use the destination
address in a packet in order to decide to which of its
neighbouring nodes the packet is to be sent. If the
destination is attached to a neighbouring node there is
no problem and the routing algorithm should always place
the packet on the queue for that destination node. When
the destination is several hops away the node may have a
choice, and this is where the routing mechanism can
choose a route that could avoid already overloaded
nodes. Criteria that could be used to base routing
decisions on include node-to-node delay times, queue
sizes, traffic rates, and hop counts.

Routing techniques are either fixed (in which the
routing tables are preset and never change), or
adaptive. Fixed routing tables may be based on previous
measurements or on simulation studies. For fixed
routing to be successful, the traffic must be
consistent; as this is not likely to happen in a large
network, adaptive routing is used in most wide area
networks. Adaptive routing uses information on network
performance to adjust the routing tables in each node
and hopefully avoid congestion by spreading the traffic
load. Adaptive routing relies on the collection of
information to change the routing tables in a sensible
way. There are three methods of collecting routing
information.

1. ISOLATED: Each node collects and uses its own information independently of the others. For instance, the current size of its output queues could be used and weighted against the number of hops needed to reach the destination by using that output link.

2. CENTRALISED: Each node collects relevant data and periodically dispatches it to a central node or control centre. The control centre processes the information from all the nodes to produce new routing tables, or updates, for each node and returns them.

3. DISTRIBUTED: Each node collects data and uses it to modify its own routing table. It also periodically exchanges that data, or its routing table, with its neighbours. As a node can only collect local information, its routing table represents its view of the network. As the routing tables are exchanged, a node can build a picture of the network.

The isolated scheme is very simple, but very naive in that a packet can be forwarded, based on local information, to a part of the network that is congested. The other two schemes involve the generation of traffic in the network that competes with the users' traffic. The centralised scheme can cause congestion at the central node which may be difficult to distinguish from real congestion, and will upset any routing decisions. The distributed scheme suffers from the problem that news travels slowly across the network. A major advantage of adaptive routing is the ability to handle node and line failures, as well as impending congestion. A failure can be treated as complete congestion as they both result in zero traffic flow. If an adaptive routing mechanism reacts too quickly, the lightly loaded part of the network becomes flooded with packets trying to avoid a loaded or failed part. If the routing mechanism reacts too slowly the problem can overtake the network and a complete blockage will occur.

A routing mechanism that has been closely studied is the ARPA network adaptive routing scheme. The primary goal of ARPA network routing is to minimise the end-to-end delay. To achieve this each IMP keeps a table showing the expected delay to every other IMP in the network and the corresponding neighbour IMP to which packets should be sent to achieve that delay. An IMP can calculate the delay between itself and each of its neighbours, either by sending a special packet to each neighbour and timing the response, or by inspecting the output queue for each neighbour.

Periodically the IMPs exchange their routing tables. When a routing table is received from a neighbour it indicates the delay from that neighbour IMP to the other IMPs; thus to calculate the delay from this IMP, the delay to that neighbour is added to each entry in the received table. Entries in the received table are then compared with the IMP's own routing table. If a lower delay entry is found in the received table, it is placed in the IMP's routing table and the neighbour that sent the table becomes the routing choice for that destination IMP.

In this way each IMP is fairly certain of using the best route with regard to delay. However if an entry in the received table is larger than the delay in the IMPs own routing table it may be that the received value is the latest value, which may have increased due to local traffic conditions in another part of the network. Using the above algorithm this proper value is ignored. Thus news of a better route is quickly accepted, but a degradation in a route is not so quickly assimilated. To overcome this resistance to 'bad news' an IMP will change to an increased delay if a number of its neighbours show increases, or if the sender of a table is already the routing choice. It is very difficult to implement a mechanism that reacts quickly enough to changes to avoid congestion and provide the best route at all times, without over-reacting and causing rapid fluctuations.

An early version of the ARPA network routing mechanism required the IMPs to exchange tables every 0.6 seconds. It was then found that the majority of the network traffic was routing table updates! IMPs now exchange their tables at a rate that depends on the traffic load and the capacity of the circuits joining the IMPs. Knowing the delay on the quickest route to reach a destination IMP does not help an IMP decide if the destination is actually accessible. To determine if the destination can be reached, IMPs also exchange tables showing the number of hops to every other IMP in the network. A very large hop count (infinity) is used to indicate that an IMP cannot be reached.

10.4 Datagrams and Virtual Circuits

The datagram and virtual circuit modes of operation were introduced in chapter 9. The X25 protocol in chapter 8 is described as a virtual call protocol, but because it only describes the host–node interface, the actual network could use either datagram or virtual call implementation. The Canadian PTT network DATAPAC uses a virtual call subnet, whereas the French network TRANSPAC uses a datagram subnet, although both use the X25 access protocol. The choices have repercussions on network efficiency, protocol implementation, routing and network control. Within the network, flexibility, which can lead to more efficient utilisation of resources, is usually more complex and therefore more expensive than a simple fixed approach.

The datagram mode of operation is very important in a general packet switched network. A large amount of the traffic that is in public packet networks involves single packet transfers. Some of the applications involved are: simple enquiries (say from a cash dispenser), electronic funds transfer and mail from one user to another. Each of these applications requires a single data packet with a possible single data packet acknowledgement. The importance of mail has been demonstrated on existing networks. A virtual call subnet will have to open a call, transfer the enquiry and the response, then close the call. For a single packet exchange, a virtual call is very inefficient. X25 now has a datagram option built into it to

accommodate the above applications, but that does not
mean the subnets will use it.

Within the network the datagram mechanism enables a
node to treat each packet separately and route it
accordingly, which allows a flexible response to changes
in the traffic load within the network. The node does
not need to keep state information for datagrams, which
saves memory space. A virtual call subnet requires a
node to decide the call route at call set up time and
use the same route throughout the call. The node keeps
state information for each call, and references each
call by a single number (the logical channel number). A
virtual call network can manage global resources much
more easily. A network accepting a call allocates
buffer space at all nodes involved in the call. The X25
level 3 call request packet has a field to specify the
class of call to be used to determine how many buffers
and how much bandwidth will be needed on this call. If
a network does not have resources at all of the nodes on
any route, the call can be refused. In a datagram
network the source node does not know the full status of
the other nodes, nor if the destination host can receive
the datagram. The packet is always accepted, subject to
local loadings. If a problem occurs or the destination
host is down, the packet may be stored for a while, or
it may be discarded to avoid cluttering the network with
undeliverable packets. In a datagram network the end-
to-end flow control has to be implemented by the hosts.
In a virtual call network a lot of the end-to-end flow
control, sequencing and error handling is handled by the
network.

From the above argument it can be seen that a virtual
call network enables easier resource management within
the network and a more functional interface for the
hosts. A datagram network is more efficient for the
single or very short packet exchanges which are expected
to provide much of the traffic on a public network.

10.5 Connecting Networks

Most existing networks use various protocols to provide their users with different services. Even new networks using X25 appear to have subtle variations in the protocol implementations. Despite the differences, there is a need to connect networks together so that a user on one network may access resources and hosts on another network. Networks are at the moment confined to a geographical area (such as a national or local network) or to a specific class of users (such as the ARPA network). Interaction between users within a network will obviously be much more frequent than interaction between users of separate networks, but the demand for inter-network operation has already been established, particularly between the PTT networks.

Connecting networks involves two problems

1. transporting the packets between two protocols

2. addressing.

The protocols used in a network fall into two groups, those used within the network (levels 1,2,3) to transfer packets from host to host, and those used between the end users (levels 4,5,6,7) to convey data in a manner appropriate to the application. The first protocol group is fixed for each network so they are network dependent. The second group of protocols is the application protocols only implemented in hosts. A network uses its own protocols to carry packets from one node to another, and an addressing mechanism to indicate the source and destination node-host pair. When two networks are joined, or concatenated, a mapping has to be made between the two network dependent protocols to take packets across the boundary. Figure 10.3 shows a situation where two networks meet. The boundary is represented by a computer known as a gateway. The gateway computer looks like a host on both networks and has a host interface on each network. The gateway takes packets from the sending network and forwards them into the receiving network. Figure 10.4 shows the protocol bridge that the gateway makes. The gateway does not

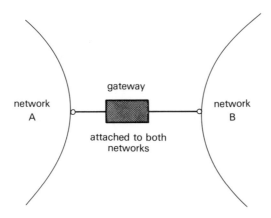

Figure 10.3 **Network Boundary and Gateway**

actually convert protocols: it receives a data packet
from the one network then takes away the network
dependent protocol layer but keeps the information (such
as addresses). It then adds the other network protocols
to be used to forward the packet. The protocol
hierarchy is very useful as it provides a clear line
between network protocols and host-to-host protocols.

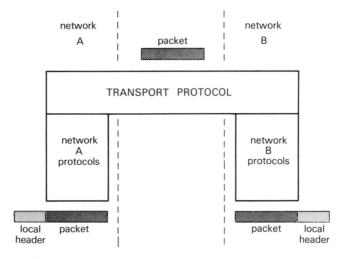

Figure 10.4 **Gateway Protocol Bridge**

The end-to-end transfer of individual packets is apparently easy: for a datagram network a gateway merely has to forward the packets independently. In a virtual call network each inter-network connection needs to be kept as a virtual call across the gateway, which requires the gateway to remember all current calls. The CCITT have defined a protocol called X75 for connecting X25-based networks. A further problem occurs where a virtual call and datagram network meet, but this is still a subject for research.

The host-to-host protocols have to be implemented on every host that wishes to communicate with another host, and this is still true of inter-network connections. The host-to-host protocols are standardised within a network, but there is a good chance that different networks will have different host protocols. A very good example of incompatibility in the applications protocols is terminal access. On the ARPA network a user would use TELNET above TCP; on PSS a user would use X3/X28/X29 above X25. Where two networks use different host-to-host protocols, there are two solutions to the incompatibility problem.

1. The user's host can have a protocol implementation for every other network protocol needed. This is a waste of resources when the number of different protocols is more than a few.

2. A protocol converter may be implemented in or near a gateway. The ·problems of conversion mean that the connection is reduced to the common facilities of both protocols.

Neither of these solutions is really acceptable. It is more likely that users will avoid the problem by inventing their own protocols, or just avoiding communication involving different protocols. A third approach is available, which is to have common applications protocols for all networks, but this has drawbacks in updating and improving the protocols as well as getting them universally accepted.

Addressing across networks presents a difficult problem that has to be met by the gateway. Each individual host, and process within that host, needs to have a unique address to identify it as a destination. Within a network an addressing scheme will be worked out that enables each node to forward a packet to the next node and for the destination node to forward the packet to the host, and finally for the host to direct the data to the correct process. This is a hierarchic addressing scheme of node, host and process so three groups of numbers would suffice. The telephone numbering system is very similar. The problem in a gateway occurs where two networks use different formats, different number ranges, or even a different hierarchic structure. Further to the addressing within the network, a host that wishes to send a message to a host in another network has to specify the other network involved, giving a fourth address field, known as the **network** field. If a host specifies a destination that is on another network, how does the local network know how to route the packets so that they reach the gateway? One answer is to introduce two levels of addressing for inter-network traffic: one level for use within the local network, known as the local address, and another, used by the gateways and hosts, known as the inter-network address.

Addressing also covers another problem, that of identifying a particular service. In the above discussion the destination process was specified as part of the address. But how does a distant user know which process is currently providing a particular service, such as file transfer, or terminal access? Two possible solutions are

1. The end-to-end protocol (transport level) specifies the service required in a special field in the connection set up packets. X25 has a field in the open request packet which is being used for this purpose.

2. Each host runs the service on a **well known** process
   address. For instance, process address 23 could be
   the terminal access server.

In (1) the source host addresses its request to the
destination host with the type of request in the packet
field, using a default process address. In (2) the
request is embedded in the addressing structure. The
gateway will have to resolve these addressing mechanisms
where networks use different arrangements.

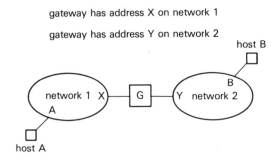

Figure 10.5 **Network Intercommunication Example**

An example of an inter-network communication is shown
in figure 10.5. Host A on network 1 wishes to
communicate to host B on network 2. Host A specifies
the inter-network address of the destination as net = 2,
host = B. The network software on the host, or the node,
recognises that it is an inter-network address (the net
number is not the local network) and looks up the
gateway to be used to reach network 2. The gateway
address is placed in the local address field of the
packet, while the inter-network address is retained
within the packet. So the local address from host A is
host X, the gateway. The local address enables the
packet to cross network 1 to the gateway which acts as a
host. The gateway takes the local network protocols off
the data packet and inspects the inter-network address.
The address of host B is now placed in the local packet
protocol for network 2 and the packet is sent across
network 2 to B. Notice that both the inter-network
address and the local network address are needed. If
the gateway discovered that the destination network was

not one to which it was attached it would forward the
packet to the next gateway. The use of an inter-network
address above the local network address implies that an
inter-network transport protocol is needed above the
local network level. In an X25 based network the
gateways are special nodes that make concatenated
virtual calls across the networks. This removes the
necessity of an inter-network layer, but gives a less
flexible mechanism.

10.6 Summary

This chapter has only touched on some of the aspects of
computer networks. It is important for a user of a
computer network to see the network as a whole system.
Knowledge of the techniques used within a network is
useful in seeing how the network may function for the
user, but all the techniques are combined to provide a
cohesive system capable of reliable operation that meets
the user's requirements.

Computer networks are very complex systems. These
will change as new techniques and ideas are evolved, and
as the user's requirements expand to make increasingly
sophisticated use of networks as tools.

Glossary

Advanced Research Projects Agency (ARPA)
An agency of the US government that initiates and funds large research projects. The agency is now known as DARPA (Defense ARPA), which indicates the application area of its research.

ASCII
(American Standards Committee for Information Interchange). In normal usage the term ASCII refers to a particular character code that is widely available on computer peripherals. The letters stand for the committee that first formulated the codes. See IA5.

asynchronous framing
A communication in which the characters are transmitted, and received, independently of each other.

Automatic Repeat Request (ARQ)
A technique used in error control that requires the receiver to request the retransmission of an message received with errors.

bandwidth
The information-carrying capacity of a channel, it is measured in hertz (Hz). The bandwidth is the difference between the highest and lowest frequencies that can be used on the channel.

base band
The frequency range in which a signal is actually generated, as opposed to the frequencies that might be used to transmit the signal after modulation.

baud
The rate at which a signal may change.

bit
The basic unit of information used in computers and digital communications.

burst
A sequence of information in a transmission; an error burst is a sequence of information that has been corrupted.

Carrier Sense Multiple Access (CSMA)
A mechanism for accessing a broadcast communication medium which tries to avoid transmission collision by not transmitting if there is already one in progress. The presence of another transmission is detected by sensing the carrier of the transmission.

CCITT
(Committee Consultatif Internationale de Telegraphique et Telephonique). An international organisation of PTTs which decides on standards for use in telecommunications. The CCITT is part of the United Nations.

channel
A path for communication. A channel connects an information source with an information receiver. The channel can be made up of several physical circuits and pieces of equipment.

check bits
The redundant information added to the end of a message to enable the receiver to check the message for possible transmission errors.

circuit
A physical connection used for communication.

common carrier
A term used in the USA to describe companies, licensed

by the Government, that provide the basic telecommunication facilities.

concentrator
A device that multiplexes several inputs onto one output (and vice versa) but uses local storage to provide a buffer against surges in traffic. A packet switched network node is a concentrator.

datagram
A packet of information, transferred in a computer network, which is independent of all other packets. The packet contains the source and destination address.

Data Communications Equipment (DCE)
The term used to describe the node in an X25 network.

Data Terminal Equipment (DTE)
The term used to describe the host in an X25 network.

EBCDIC
(Extended Binary Coded Decimal Interchange Code). The name given to the character code used on IBM computers.

forward error correction
A technique used in error control, in which a large amount of redundant information is added to the message so that error correction can be done by the receiver.

Frequency Division Multiplexing (FDM)
A technique for multiplexing a channel by dividing the frequency range.

frequency shift keying (FSK)
A modulation technique in which digital signals are coded directly into frequencies.

Front End Computer (FEC)
A small (mini or micro) computer used to handle communications devices for a large general purpose computer.

gateway
In computer networks a gateway is a computer that is connected to two or more networks and allows traffic to flow between the networks.

host
A user computer on a network.

IA5
(International Alphabet number 5). A standard character code of the ISO that closely resembles ASCII.

Interface Message Processor (IMP)
A node computer on the ARPA network.

MODEM
(MOdulator-DEModulator). The piece of equipment that allows digital communication signals to be transferred over the PSTN by modulation.

modulation
A technique used in communications to change a base band information signal into a signal more suitable for a particular medium.

multiplexing
A mechanism for using a single communications channel to carry the signals from a number of other channels.

node
A computer in a packet switching network that does the store and forward switching. The node is usually separate from the host.

noise
The extra signals that are always received on a circuit that can cause errors in the received information.

packet switching
Messages from the user computers (hosts) are broken into small packets. These packets are then switched from node to node in a network to reach the destination host.

Packet Switching Service (PSS)
The public packet switching network in the UK run by British Telecom. PSS uses X25 as its access protocol.

parity
An error-detecting mechanism; often used on single characters. The bits of a character are summed and an extra bit added either to make the total number of 1s even (even parity) or odd (odd parity).

piggy-back
A mechanism used in flow control where acknowledgements are added to data messages using the reverse channel.

private circuit
A PSTN connection between two sites that bypasses the dialling equipment in the exchange. Thus the circuit can only be used for communication between the two sites but should have a lower error rate than a switched circuit.

protocol
An agreed format for communication between two or more parties.

PSTN
The Public Switched Telephone network.

PTT
(Postal, Telegraph and Telephone authority). The administration that runs the posts and all public telecommunication systems in a country. In Europe these are all government monopolies. In the USA the PTTs are private companies (common carriers).

redundancy
Extra information that is added to a message, it is an overhead on the channel to carry the extra information. The extra information is used to implement a protocol.

RS232C
The name given the the physical terminal interface standard V24 in the USA.

store and forward
The technique, used in nodes, whereby messages (or packets) are stored in the node memory before being forwarded on a communication channel.

synchronous framing
A communication in which the characters follow one another immediately, thus the receiver and sender need to have synchronised clocks.

time division multiplexing (TDM)
A technique for sharing the capacity of a channel by dividing it into slots of equal time.

V24
A standard interface for connecting asynchronous character equipment. It is equivalent to the EIA RS232C standard.

virtual call
An end-to-end connection between two hosts across a packet switched network in which information can be exchanged in a sequenced flow controlled manner. Addressing information is only used when the call is set up.

Bibliography

Davies, D.W. and Barber, D.L.A.
Communication Networks for Computers, Wiley 1973.

Davies, D.W., Barber, D.L.A., Price, W.L., Solomides, C.M.
Computer Networks and Their Protocols, Wiley 1980.

These two books are considered together as they form the most consistent, and so far the most comprehensive study of computer communications. The first volume contains technical details of a number of communication mechanisms, with the emphasis on the networks that were available in 1973. The second volume is concerned entirely with computer networks. Both are recommended to any serious student of computer communications. There is a good emphasis on CCITT standards.

Doll, Dixon R.
Data Communications: Facilities, Networks, and Systems Design, Wiley 1978.

This book was written by an American for the American DP manager and student, but as the terminal market is dominated by the US standards and systems the book is good for the reader who is interested in the material covered in chapters 3 to 6 of this book. There is a good discussion of the problems in designing terminal networks in the DP environment.

Kuo, F.F. (Ed)
Protocols and Techniques for Data Communication Networks, Prentice-Hall 1981.

A number of leading American researchers have contributed chapters to this book. The subject matter of the various chapters is somewhat disjointed, but the authors have tried to relate to each other's chapters

where possible. Most of the authors turn to the ARPA
network for examples. Chapters of particular interest
as further reading are on: background, transport
protocols, terminal and file transfer protocols, routing
and flow control, broadcast satellite networks.

McNamara, T.E.
Technical Aspects of Data Communication, Digital
Equipment Corporation, 1977

This book is mostly concerned with the electrical signal
level of computer communications. However there are
detailed comparisons of the CCITT and EIA standards at
this level, in particular V24 and RS232.

Post Offic/NCC
Handbook of Data Communications, NCC 1975.

This book covers the technical details of chapters 2 and
3 in some depth. The text is only of relevance to UK
readers, or others interested in a pure PTT PSTN.

Schwartz, M
Computer Communication Network Design and Analysis,
Prentice-Hall 1977.

A detailed study of the theory of communication network
design with mathematical analysis. The optimising
techniques for routing and flow control in networks are
covered with worked examples. The text is particularly
good on the design of terminal networks, as opposed to
switched computer networks.

Tannenbaum, A.
Computer Networks, Prentice-Hall 1981

This book covers the protocols used in packet switching
networks. The author has arranged the text to follow
the ISO protocol hierarchy, as far as possible. A very
good mix of commercial, PTT and DARPA protocols are
covered in some detail.

<u>Papers</u>

These are of special relevence as further reading.

Cerf,V.G. and Kahn,R.E
A protocol for packet network interconnection. IEEE transactions on Communication Technology; vol COM-22 1974 pp637-641.

This paper introduces the TCP protocol discussed in chapter 9.

Metcalfe, R. and Boggs, D.
Ethernet: Distributed packet switching for local computer networks. Communications of the ACM, vol 19, no 7, July 1976

This paper describes the Ethernet local area network covered in chapter 7.

Proceedings of IEEE – Special Issue on Packet Switching
Vol 66, no 11, November 1978

This special issue contains a number of papers specially written by American researchers as a technical introduction to the various aspects of packet switching. Many of the examples are taken from the ARPA network, but this reflects the background of the authors. A number of papers also consider PTT network problems. Some particularly interesting papers include: Evolution of Packet Switching, written by Roberts, this is a very readable history of packet switching. Papers on packet radio and satellite networks describe existing networks and their protocols. The paper by Clark, et al, on Local Area Networks gives a good background to the technology and protocols of these networks.

Index